BRISTOL BAY

A SOCIOECONOMIC STUDY

David T. Kresge
Susan R. Fison
Anthony F. Gasbarro

Institute of Social, Economic and Government Research
University of Alaska

Library of Congress Catalogue No. 74-620052
ISBN 0-88353-013-9
Series: ISEGR Report No. 41

Published by
Institute of Social, Economic and Government Research
University of Alaska
Fairbanks, Alaska
1974

PREFACE

This report, which is designed to provide a comprehensive socio-economic description of the Bristol Bay region, was originally prepared as a part of a larger report, "The Bristol Bay Environment, a Background Study of Available Knowledge." The original study was performed for the Army Corps of Engineers by the University of Alaska's Institute of Social, Economic and Government Research at Fairbanks and the Arctic Environmental Information and Data Center at Anchorage. Its purpose was to provide background information for possible inclusion in environmental impact statements relating to petroleum development in Bristol Bay.

ISEGR is publishing this revised portion of the original report as part of its Man in the Arctic Program. The Man in the Arctic Program, funded by the National Science Foundation, is a long-range research effort intended to develop a basic understanding of the forces of change in Alaska and to apply this understanding in dealing with the critical problems of social and economic development. We believe that the socioeconomic information on Bristol Bay presented here has an immediate relevance and is of potential utility to many persons involved in public and private decision-making in the region and in Alaska generally. In addition, ISEGR has chosen Bristol Bay as a region in which further intensive research will be carried out under the Man in the Arctic Program. This report, as a compilation of the available current information and historical data, will serve as a baseline for further studies in which socioeconomic data not presently available will be compiled and analyzed.

*   *   *

We would like to express special appreciation to those Bristol Bay residents who provided support and information for the study. Notable among these were Nels Anderson, President of the Bristol Bay Native Corporation; Sam Coxson, Dillingham City Manager; Jay Hammond, Chairman of the Bristol Bay Borough; and Tom Armour, Borough Manager.

George Rogers, ISEGR economist, reviewed and criticized the manuscript. His unpublished work, "A Study of the Socioeconomic Impact of Change in Harvesting Labor Force in Bristol Bay," proved to be an invaluable source of information. Ron Evans guided our use of 1970 census data and arranged for special computer tabulations. Earlene Goodwin compiled statistical information and tables. Bebe Brannock and Helen Lewis provided administrative support and prepared the manuscript.

Ronald Crowe had responsibility for editing and preparing this report for publication, with production assistance from Wendy Anderson and Lavonia Wiele.

David T. Kresge, Director
Man in the Arctic Program

Victor Fischer, Director
Institute of Social, Economic and Government Research

TABLE OF CONTENTS

CHAPTER FIVE. HOUSING AND PUBLIC SERVICES

CHAPTER SIX. INDUSTRIAL ACTIVITY

CHAPTER SEVEN. TRANSPORTATION FACILITIES AND COSTS

CHAPTER EIGHT. LAND USE AND LAND STATUS

LIST OF FIGURES

LIST OF MAPS

CHAPTER 1
GENERAL DESCRIPTION
OF THE STUDY REGION

Overview

The Bristol Bay region is a mountain-bordered basin in the southwest corner of Alaska on the southern coast of the Bering Sea. The basin opens away from the state's population centers and shipping lanes, making it one of the most isolated areas in Alaska. Sitting between the Kuskokwim Mountains to the west and north and the Aleutian Range to the south and east, this basin forms the watershed for the river and lake systems that supports the tremendously valuable Bristol Bay salmon fishery. For present purposes, we will define the study region as the area encompassed by the Bristol Bay Borough and the surrounding Bristol Bay Census Division (see Figure 1-1).

A recent study by Rogers provides an excellent summary of the economic history of this region.

> ... In aboriginal times it was inhabited by four major Eskimo tribes living on salmon, sea mammals and upriver land mammals. Fisheries and fur resources have been the source of income and employment in the region from the beginning of "historic time" until the present with the addition of some defense and other government spending. The Wood and Nushagak Rivers were prodigious breeding grounds for beaver, mink and muskrat and the fur trade was the first source of outside contact and commercial development.
>
> The first salmon cannery was erected near the Moravian mission at Carmel in 1884 followed by the rapid multiplication of plant and gear engaged in the harvesting and canning of the sal-

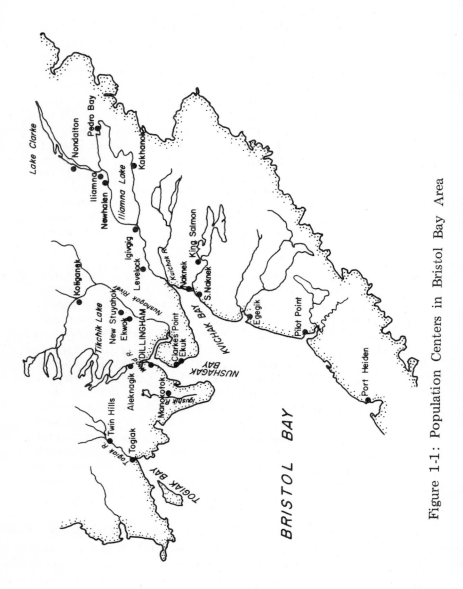

Figure 1-1: Population Centers in Bristol Bay Area

mon runs of the Bay. Until recently, this commercial exploitation
of the region's principal resource supported little permanent local
economic activity. Initially the total shore work force was made
up of Chinese transported by sailing ships from San Francisco
each season along with cannery supplies and returned with the
canned salmon pack. Fishermen were Italians and Scandinavians
from California and the Pacific Northwest. Some residents began
to become involved in the 1920's and after. A special 1939 study
of employment and income in the region's salmon fisheries reported that of 8,227 employed in the industry at that date 496
were Natives and 1,387 non-Native residents of Alaska. No indication was given of how many of these last were residents of the
region. Fifteen years later another report stated "of a total of
about 6,000 men presently employed in the fishing industry in
the Bristol Bay area, 4,000 are brought in from the United States;
1,000 are recruited from other parts of the Territory; and only
1,000 are provided locally."

Other marine resources are abundantly present in the region,
but exploitation of these has been minimal because of the re-
moteness of the region from markets and sources of supply.
Tourism and outdoor recreation potential remain underdevel-
oped. Fur harvests today are minor in importance. There are
some indications of mineral potential, but development has been
minor and sporadic with some petroleum exploration during the
last decade. The advent of World War II brought the establishment of a permanent defense base at King Salmon near Naknek
and temporary smaller stations elsewhere. For the most part, the
residents of the region have continued to follow a subsistence
existence supplemented by cash income employment in commercial salmon fishing and welfare. None of these developments
brought any change in the basic transportation systems of the
region beyond defense stimulated improvement in air service and
some minor road extensions.[1]

In 1970, there were about 4,600 persons living in the Bristol
Bay region (see Table 1-1). About one-third of the population is
white and two-thirds are Native. Eskimos are the largest Native group
and account for nearly 60 percent of the Native population. Much of

---

[1] George W. Rogers, "A Study of the Socio-Economic Impact of Changes in the
Harvesting Labor Force in the Alaska Salmon Industry," unpublished (Fair-
banks: University of Alaska, Institute of Social, Economic and Government
Research, December 1972) pp. 34-36.

Table 1-1
SUMMARY STATISTICS, 1960 and 1970

	1960	1970		
	Bristol Bay	Bristol Bay Borough	Bristol Bay Division	Total
Population	4,024	1,147	3,485	4,632
White	1,423	922	671	1,593
Native	⎡	186	2,763	2,949
Eskimo	2,601	35	1,656	1,691
Other	⎣	39	51	90
Military Personnel	536	434	5	439
Civilian Labor Force	657	224	658	882
Employment	514	165	584	749
Private	309	54	298	352
Government	205	111	286	397
Unemployment	143	59	74	133
Rate (percent)	21.8	26.3	11.2	15.1
Median Family Income	$5,955	$12,390	$6,671	$7,784

Sources: U.S. Department of Commerce, Bureau of the Census, *1960 Census*, Alaska, Tables 27, 83, 84 and 86; *1970 Census*, Alaska, Tables 121 and 124; James D. Babb, Jr., "Age and Sex Characteristics of Alaskas Population," *Alaska Review of Business and Economic Conditions*, Vol. 9, No. 1 (Fairbanks: Institute of Social, Economic and Government Research, 1972) Table 5.

the non-Native population is concentrated around the King Salmon Air Force Base within the Bristol Bay Borough.

As shown in Figure 1-1 and Table 1-2, the population is scattered throughout the region in over twenty small towns and villages. Dillingham and the Bristol Bay Borough are the only two concentrations of population, and together they account for less than half of the region's population. Furthermore, there is no indication in these two areas of increasing concentration over time. If anything, the reverse is true; several of the remote areas are growing more rapidly than the relatively urbanized areas. This dispersion of settlements may simply reflect individual preference or it may be necessitated by the economy's continued reliance on subsistence activities. Given the nature of the environment, subsistence activities require large land areas around each settlement. It may be that more concentrated settlement is not feasible under present conditions.

The only significant source of private employment in the region is provided by the fishing industry during the annual salmon runs. Since these runs last only about six weeks, the extreme seasonality of the fishing industry makes it very difficult to describe employment patterns accurately. For example, the average annual employment during 1970 was about 450 in commercial fishing and about 700 in fish processing. But in July of that year, at the peak of the salmon run, there were 3,000 persons employed in commercial fishing and another 3,300 were working in the canneries.[2] A substantial number of these people engaged in seasonal employment come from outside the Bristol Bay region and leave for other jobs when the season is over. For local residents, however, the fishing season may offer the only employment of the entire year. At the end of the season, the Bristol Bay Natives collect their wages, return to their villages from the fishing camps and simply drop out of the labor force until the next season.

Since the census data shown in Table 1-1 were collected in late March or early April of 1970, they provide useful information on the pattern of permanent, or year-round, employment. It is apparent

_____

[2]Ibid., p. 40.

Table 1-2
COMMUNITY SIZE
BRISTOL BAY 1970

900 or more population	Population
Dillingham	914
300 – 899 population	
King Salmon AFB	403
Naknek	318
Togiak	388
200 – 299 population	
Manokotak	214
New Stuyahok	216
100 – 199 population	
Aleknagik	219
Egegik	153
Ekwok	103
Nondalton	184
South Naknek	154
25 – 100 population	
Clarks Point	95
Ekuk	51
Igiugig	36
Iliamna	58
Kakhonak	88
Levelock	98
Newhalen	88
Pedro Bay	65
Pilot Point	68
Port Heiden	81
Twin Hills	67

Sources: U.S. Department of Commerce, Bureau of the Census, *1970 Census Alaska*, Table 6; *1970 Census*, Alaska, special computer runs.

that the government sector is the major source of permanent employment. Government jobs account for over half of the total, and if the military were included, the proportion employed by the government would rise to 70 percent of the workforce. In the private sector, the local canneries provide a small amount of permanent employment. Also, the transport sector provides crucial air services to the region throughout the winter, and thus is an important year-round employer.

The median family income in Bristol Bay is $7,800 as compared to $12,400 for the state as a whole. Due to the influence of the King Salmon Air Force Base, income in Bristol Bay Borough is about the same as the state average. In the Bristol Bay Division, however, median family income is $6,700, only slightly more than half of the state average. In addition, the difficulty of getting supplies to Bristol Bay substantially raises the cost of living in the region. Thus, the relative gap in real incomes is even larger than that shown by cash money income. Because of the high cost of living and the relatively low incomes, it seems clear that subsistence activities are necessary in the Bristol Bay region to augment cash incomes.

Major Communities in Bristol Bay

The communities in Bristol Bay included in the 1970 census are listed in Table 1-2 and shown on Map 1-1. In discussing these communities, it is helpful to combine them into six groups on the basis of geographic and economic linkages. The first group consists of the villages around Nushagak Bay and centers on Dillingham, the largest city in Bristol Bay. Dillingham also serves as the commercial center for the second group, the Nushagak River villages of Koliganek, New Stuyahok, and Ekwok. In terms of fishing activity and trade, these villages might be regarded as part of the general Dillingham area. However, on the basis of other socioeconomic characteristics, particularly population growth, they display a distinctly different pattern and need to be treated separately.

The next major group contains Naknek, South Naknek, and King Salmon, which are linked through the governmental structure of Bristol Bay Borough as well as through economic ties. The seven villages in the fourth group are located around Iliamna Lake. For much of the year, they are relatively isolated from the rest of Bristol Bay, but during the summer, fishing activities and trade bring them in close contact with the Naknek region.

The two remaining groups are located at the extreme western and southern corners of Bristol Bay. Togiak and the nearby village of Twin Hills carry on trade with Dillingham, but the development pattern seems quite independent of the rest of the Bristol Bay region. In particular, Togiak has been growing rapidly despite an almost complete absence of the public facilities usually found in growing communities. The final group of villages contains those located on the Alaska Peninsula: Levelock, Egegik, Pilot Point, and Port Heiden. These are all essentially fishing villages with stable populations.

In general, the study region is the same as the region encompassed by the Bristol Bay Native Corporation. However, the Corporation does include several communities (Chignik, Chignik Lagoon, Chignik Lake, Ivanof Bay, and Perryville) which are located on the south side of the Alaska Peninsula. Because these communities are well outside the geographic region being studied, they have not been included in the discussion below.

Dillingham and Nushagak Bay Villages

Dillingham, with a 1970 population of 914, is the largest community in Bristol Bay (see Table 1-2 and Figure 1-1). It is located 350 air miles southwest of Anchorage at the extreme northern end of Nushagak Bay near the mouths of the Nushagak and Wood Rivers. Nushagak Bay flows into Bristol Bay about thirty-five miles to the south.

In 1818, Russians established a post in the Bristol Bay region on the east side of Nushagak Bay. By 1822, an active fur trade was being carried on through this post. The population in the area grew, and the fur trade continued after the U.S. purchased Alaska in 1867.

The first salmon cannery in Bristol Bay was established in 1884 at the same location as the fur trading post. Two more canneries were built in the next two years, but these were located on the west side of Nushagak Bay in the vicinity of the present town of Dillingham. In the following years, more canneries were built and between 1908 and 1910 there were ten canneries operating on Nushagak Bay. The town of Dillingham was officially named in 1904 for William Paul Dillingham, a U.S. Senator who conducted the first comprehensive investigation of Alaska by a congressional committee.

The population of Dillingham reached 280 by 1939 and was double that by 1950. Population declined between 1950 and 1960 but then shot up to more than 900 persons in 1970. However, much of the increase shown in the 1970 census occurred in 1963 when the city of Dillingham incorporated over a twenty-two square-mile area. As a result of this expansion, the city absorbed the populations of the nearby settlements of Kanakanak, Nelsonville, and Wood River Village. The incorporation also added to the population of Dillingham all the households residing along the roads leading to those villages. If the 1960 census had encompassed a comparable area, Dillingham's 1960 population would have been about 800 persons.[3]

Natives account for 64 percent of Dillingham's population, with Aleuts comprising the largest single racial group, or about 42 percent of the population. Whites make up the next largest group with 33 percent or 325 persons. The remaining 22 percent breaks down into Eskimos, Indians, and others. During the summer fishing season, the population in the Dillingham area may double as residents of the Nushagak Bay and Nushagak River villages come to Dillingham for the salmon season.[4] During this time, many of these people live in established summer camps on the outskirts of town.

Historically, Dillingham's growth has been closely linked to the development of the salmon canning industry. In recent years, Dillingham has also come to serve as a regional center for trade and services.

_____

[3] Alaska State Housing Authority, *City of Dillingham Comprehensive Plan*, (Anchorage: June 1972) p. 33.

[4] James W. Van Stone, *Eskimos of the Nushagak River*, Publications in Anthropology, Vol. 15, 1967 (Seattle: University of Washington) p. 155.

Kodiak Western Alaska Airlines, a local carrier which serves most of the villages of the region, operates out of Dillingham, thus making the city a transfer point for passenger and freight traffic. Wien Air Alaska also provides service connecting Dillingham to Anchorage as well as to other communities in the Bristol Bay region. In addition, several charter flying services operate out of the city.

As the regional commercial center, Dillingham has general merchandise stores, a hardware store, a lumber yard, a bank, food stores, liquor stores, and a post office. It also has such recreational facilities as a movie theater and pool halls. It offers the services of hotels, restaurants, and bars.

Dillingham has more extensive community facilities and services than any other population center in the area. Its facilities and services include:

- A water and sewer system (completed in 1964).

- A high school (completed in 1961).

- A small boat harbor (completed in 1962).

- Local and long-distance telephone service.

- An electric generating plant.

- A public health service hospital (at Kanakanak), a public health nurse in residence (at Dillingham), and a private practitioner.

The economy of Dillingham is significantly strengthened by a substantial amount of employment in various government agencies. These agencies include the Federal Aviation Administration, the U.S. Fish and Wildlife Service, the Alaska Department of Fish and Game, the Alaska Department of Highways, the city school district, and the U.S. Public Health Service Hospital at Kanakanak. The employment and income generated by these agencies is particularly important; in contrast to employment in the fishing industry, it is stable with little seasonal variation. In addition, unlike many areas in Alaska, government employment in Dillingham is entirely civilian; there are no military bases in the area.

The communities around Nushagak Bay include Aleknagik, Manokotak, Clark's Point, and Ekuk. Due to the economic ties through commercial fishing activities and geographic proximity, Dillingham serves as the commercial center for all these villages. Aleknagik has particularly close ties with Dillingham because the two communities are connected by a twenty-four mile long road. The village is located north of Dillingham on Lake Aleknagik, the southernmost of the five lakes in the Wood River lake system. The Eskimo population was virtually wiped out by an influenza epidemic in 1918-1919. Beginning in about 1928, families began to move back into the area.[5] Population grew steadily, reaching a peak of 231 in the 1960 census, but then dropped to 219 by 1970. Presently about 70 percent of the residents are Eskimo, and most of the other residents are whites. The only significant source of employment for the Aleknagik Natives is the Bristol Bay salmon fishery. During the salmon runs, almost the entire Native population moves to various fish camps to work on the fishing boats, to set nets, or to work in the canneries. The non-Native families in Aleknagik are generally employed as school teachers, postmaster, and business owner/operators.

Manokotak is a rapidly growing Eskimo community about twenty-five miles southwest of Dillingham where the Igushik River empties into Nushagak Bay. All but a few of the 214 residents of Manokotak are Eskimo. A 1966 Bureau of Indian Affairs study observed that:

> One of the Eskimo dialects is used almost exclusively for communication among the people. Most often English interpreters are needed for meetings with government officials. English is taught in the school but is little used at home.[6]

---

[5] Ibid., pp. 155-156.

[6] U.S. Department of the Interior, Bureau of Indian Affairs, *Manokotak, Alaska—Village Study* (August 1966) pp. 5-6.

Commercial fishing in Nushagak Bay provides the major source of income and, until recently, almost all goods were brought from Dillingham by boat in the summer. In 1969, a village cooperative store began operation, purchasing goods directly from Seattle. More than half of the village houses were replaced with new units in 1971,[7] and plans are being made to provide electric power for the village.

Clarks Point and Ekuk are located about two miles apart on the opposite side of Nushagak Bay from (and to the south of) Dillingham. Although Ekuk was once an Eskimo village, both it and Clarks Point are now mainly cannery towns. In recent years, only the cannery in Ekuk has been operating. Although the summer population is quite substantial due to the fishing camps in the area, the population reported in the 1970 census is only ninety-five for Clarks Point and fifty-one for Ekuk. In general, the permanent population seems to be declining, and Clarks Point has petitioned to be moved to a new site because of recurrent flooding problems.

Nushagak River Villages

The Nushagak River villages of Koliganek, New Stuyahok, Ekwok, and Portage Creek had a total population of roughly 520 at the time of the 1970 census. However, the population of the individual villages has fluctuated a great deal because of the mobile population in the Nushagak River region. Some families move to Nushagak Bay for several years and then return, and it is not uncommon for a family to maintain a cabin in more than one community. As a whole, the river villages grew by nearly 50 percent between 1960 and 1970. It appears that during recent years these villages have been drawing families from the communities located on the coast of Nushagak Bay.[8]

Koliganek: Koliganek, with a 1970 population of 142, is the

---

[7]Federal Field Committee for Development Planning in Alaska, *Community Inventory* (Anchorage: 1971) p. 120.

[8]Van Stone, *Eskimos*, pp. 144-150.

village located farthest up the Nushagak River. The present village site was just established in 1964 and is the third location for the village, although it is only seven miles from the original site and three miles from the previous location. Until recently almost all supplies were brought during the summer by boat from Dillingham, a trip which required three days or more depending on shifting sand bars and water flow in the Nushagak River. The residents established a cooperative store there in 1970 which has succeeded in reducing prices of goods in the village by approximately 15 percent.[9] The population is mostly Eskimo, and despite the lack of employment opportunities, the village grew by more than 40 percent between 1960 and 1970. However, this increase may have been partially caused by the new school that was constructed by the Bureau of Indian Affairs in 1965. Except for some trapping and a few temporary jobs, the only source of income and employment is the salmon fishery in Bristol Bay.

New Stuyahok: New Stuyahok is a rapidly growing community on the Nushagak River about forty miles below Koliganek and about fifty-two air miles northeast of Dillingham. Nearly all of the 216 residents are Eskimo, and the spoken language is mainly Eskimo; English is used only when necessary. Like the other villages in the region, New Stuyahok's economy depends almost entirely on commercial fishing in Bristol Bay. However, the village has a relatively high level of services and facilities. A large school was constructed in 1960, and a post office was established in 1961. The village has electricity and recently the U.S. Public Health Service put in a sewerage system.[10] Before 1971, many of the homes in the village were considered substandard, but during that year over half of the housing units were replaced by new ones.[11] In 1970, the village established a

---

[9] Community Enterprise Development Corporation, Contract Renewal—December 1972 (Anchorage: 1972) p. V-45.

[10] Timothy J. Rogers, "Bristol Bay Native corporation Presentation to Senate Public Works Subcommittee on Water Resources " (August 8, 1973) p. 19.

[11] Community Inventory, p. 38.

cooperative store and succeeded in reducing prices to consumers by about 25 percent.[12]

Ekwok: In contrast to the other river villages, the population of Ekwok seems to be holding constant or perhaps declining slightly. There are about 100 persons in the village, a third of whom are Aleut and most of the others are Eskimo. Since there are no stores in Ekwok, all supplies come from Dillingham, about forty miles southwest of the village. Except for a small school and a post office, Ekwok has no community facilities.

Although the 1970 census does not include Portage Creek, the population of this village is estimated to be at least sixty persons.[13] Located about thirty miles from Dillingham, the village is the most accessible of the Nushagak River communities. Many of the residents of Portage Creek have moved there from Koliganek and Dillingham.[14] The village location seems attractive to those who do not want to live in Dillingham but yet do not want to be too far away from the city's services.

Bristol Bay Borough

The communities of Naknek, South Naknek and King Salmon comprise the Bristol Bay Borough, a 1,200-square-mile area in the Kvichak Bay region. Naknek is located on the north bank of the Naknek River near the point where it empties into Kvichak Bay. South Naknek is situated one mile south on the other side of the Naknek River. King Salmon and the Air Force Station are about fifteen miles east of Naknek.

------

[12]CEDC, p. V-63.

[13]Bristol Bay Native Corporation, "Presentation to Senate Public Works Sub-committee on Water Resources—August 1973," p. 21, gives the population as sixty. *Dillingham Comprehensive Plan*, 1971, p. 33, estimates the population as seventy. The application submitted in November 1970 for incorporation as a fourth class city gives the population as ninety.

[14]Van Stone, *Eskimos*, p. 150.

The local economy of the twin communities of Naknek and South Naknek is based almost exclusively upon the salmon industry. The first salmon cannery began operations near Naknek in 1890. Then, as the Naknek-Kvichak River region came to be recognized as one of the most abundant sources of red salmon in Bristol Bay, other canneries were built.

The harvesting of salmon took place only a few weeks each year, but some of the seasonal residents soon made the area adjacent to the canneries their permanent home. As the cannery towns of Naknek and South Naknek grew, they drew their populations from many other areas. In a 1966 survey of heads of households, the Bureau of Indian Affairs found that:

- 25 percent were born locally.

- 25 percent came from outside Alaska.

- 42 percent were from villages within a fifty-mile radius of Naknek.

- 8 percent were from other villages within Alaska.[15]

Today the residents represent a diverse ethnic mixture of white, Eskimo, Aleut, and Indian. Over the years, the racial lines have been blurred even further by intermarriage.[16]

The 1970 census enumerated 1,147 persons within the boundaries of Bristol Bay Borough. Of these, 403 were military personnel stationed at King Salmon Air Force Base. The civilian population of King Salmon is about 200 persons, and there are 150 persons in South Naknek. Naknek, the largest nonmilitary community in the Bristol Bay Borough, has a population of nearly 320 persons.

---

[15]U.S. Department of the Interior, Bureau of Indian Affairs, *Naknek and S. Naknek — Village Study* (August 1966) pp. 3-6.

[16]Ibid., p. 17.

Naknek: Naknek is the center of fishing and canning activities for the Borough. it is also the point through which most supplies are hauled in and through which the salmon pack is carried to outside markets. Following the construction of a road between Naknek and King Salmon airport in 1949, Naknek became clearly established as the trade center for the Kvichak Bay area. Later, government agencies were based in the community, and when the Borough was formed, Naknek became the seat of local government for the region. At present, Naknek offers the highest concentration of goods and services in this portion of Bristol Bay. It has a general store, a hotel, several restaurants, fuel distributors, a civic center, and recreational facilities. Electric power is supplied by a local cooperative, but as yet, there is no community water and sewer system. The Borough school system covering kindergarten through high school, is head-quartered in Naknek. A Public Health Service district nurse maintains an office in Naknek that serves most of the Alaska Peninsula as well as the Borough.

South Naknek: In contrast to Naknek, South Naknek has grown slowly. The population in 1970 was 154, as compared to 134 in 1939. A major deterrent to development has been the Naknek River, which separates South Naknek from the bulk of the population and from the economic activity in the rest of the Borough. This sharply curtails South Naknek's access to trade facilities and public services. The school in the village is only an elementary school. High school students from South Naknek must commute by an "air school bus" to attend the school in Naknek.[17] South Naknek has a meeting hall, a post office, and a small airstrip. Electric power is available from the plant in Naknek. Of the three communities in the Borough, South Naknek has the least adequate housing. A substantial portion of the housing is overcrowded, has inadequate facilities, and is of poor structural quality.[18]

King Salmon: The third community in the Borough, King Sal-

---

[17] Jay Hammond, chairman of Bristol Bay Borough, personal communication, December 1973.

[18] USDI, *Naknek Village Study*, pp. 14-15.

mon, depends almost entirely upon the activities of the various federal and state agencies located there. The most important of these is the King Salmon Air Force Base. The site of what is now King Salmon was first surveyed by the Civil Aeronautics Administration (now the Federal Aviation Agency) in 1941.[19] The CAA acquired 3,845 acres of land and began construction of an airfield and requisite support facilities. When the United States entered World War II at the close of 1941, the Army assumed control of the airfield. During the war, the airfield, named Naknek Army Air Base, was a fuel stop, weather information point, and rest stop. After the war the government placed the base on inactive status and the CAA took over administration of the facility. In 1947, the government renamed the facility King Salmon Air Force Base and put it into operation as a satellite base of Elmendorf Air Force Base. The new station was part of a network of mainland bases to be used in the air defense of Alaska. The King Salmon Station was to serve as an advanced staging field on the Alaska Peninsula from the mainland to Aleutian Island stations.

In 1949, the Army Corps of Engineers built a road to connect the King Salmon Air Force Station with Naknek. The road, now maintained by the state, links King Salmon air transportation facilities with most of Bristol Bay Borough's population. The new road greatly increased the accessibility of the area to air transportation and played a major role in facilitating the future growth and development of the area.

During the 1950's, King Salmon continued to develop. Construction was begun on an Alaska Coast and Weather (AC&W) station in 1951, and a $10 million modernization of the facility was completed in 1955. Today King Salmon is a forward fighter base and an alternate landing site for Elmendorf Air Force Base.

King Salmon has a total population of 605 of which 403 are military personnel stationed on the Air Force site, and the remainder are largely government employees of the Federal Aviation Agency,

---

[19]U.S. Air Force, *King Salmon*, information brochure supplied by the 5071st Air Base Squadron at King Salmon Airport, 1973.

Weather Bureau, Alaska Department of Fish and Game, National Park Service, and U.S. Fish and Wildlife Service. Both the civilian and military populations are highly transient. King Salmon is classified as a remote duty site and most military personnel are stationed there for only one year. The tenure of government personnel with the various agencies averages two years.[20] Ninety-four percent of the civilian population of 202 are white. The few Natives who live in the community are government employees and their dependents.

Lake Iliamna and Vicinity

About 550 persons live in seven scattered villages in the Lake Iliamna area: Nondalton, Iliamna, Newhalen, Pedro Bay, Kakhanok, Port Alsworth, and Igiugig (see Table 1-2). The village of Iliamna is the only predominately white settlement. Most of its residents are Federal Aviation Agency employees and their dependents stationed at the Iliamna Airport.[21] Of fifty-eight persons living in the village in 1970, thirty-five were white and twenty-three were Native, most of whom were Indian.

The Iliamna Lake region is the only area in Bristol Bay with a significant Indian population. The northeastern end of the lake has been inhabited by Tanaina Athabascans since aboriginal times.[22] Nondalton, with a population of 184, is the largest village in the Iliamna area and the largest Indian village in Bristol Bay. The other Indian village is Pedro Bay, a community of sixty-five persons on the eastern end of the lake. All of the eighty-eight residents of Kakhanok on the southern shore of the lake are Eskimos. The other predominantly Eskimo village is Igiugig, with a population of thirty-six, which is located on the western end of the lake. The residents of Newhalen, population eighty-eight, are primarily Aleuts. Between

---

[20]*Naknek Community Survey.*

[21]Iliamna-Newhalen Community Survey by Itinerant Public Health Nurse, 1966.

[22]Wendall H. Oswalt, *Alaskan Eskimos* (Scranton, Pennsylvania: Chandler Publishing Company, 1967) Map 2.

1950 and 1960, the total population of the Iliamna Lake region increased 67 percent. However, much of this increase was caused by military personnel being stationed at Nondalton. Between 1950 and 1960 the civilian population increased by only 26 percent. In the 1960's, the overall population of the Iliamna region dropped 9 percent, but the civilian population actually increased by about 18 percent. All of the villages except Port Alsworth and Nondalton appear to have had moderate population increases between 1960 and 1970. Because its population was less than twenty-five, Port Alsworth was not included in the 1970 census publications.

Many of the settlements have developed long-standing ties. Newhalen and Iliamna are five miles apart, but they are connected by a road and share the same school, airport, and store.[23] Each year, many Iliamna residents migrate to the shores of Bristol Bay for the salmon runs. A large proportion of them move to the Kvichak Bay area communities, particularly Naknek, for employment as commercial fishermen or cannery workers. In addition to this seasonal cash employment, nearly all Iliamna villagers depend heavily on subsistence activities.[24]

Supplies for the Iliamna Lake region have to be brought in by air or, during the summer, by boat. Despite the high cost of air freight, this is the only means of acquiring supplies during much of the year. When water shipment is feasible, goods come up the Kvichak River from Naknek or from Iliamna Bay on the Cook Inlet coast. The goods landed at Iliamna Bay must be trucked over the fifteen-mile portage road to Iliamna Lake. This road is primitive and traverses very rugged terrain.[25] In sum, the relative inaccessibility of the villages around Iliamna Lake makes obtaining supplies difficult

---

[23] Iliamna-Newhalen Community Survey.

[24] U.S. Department of the Interior, Bureau of Indian Affairs, *Nondalton, Alaska — Village Study, August 1966.*

[25] Alaska, Department of Highways, *Peninsula Crossing — Socio-Economic Study, 1969.*

and adds substantially to the cost of living.

Togiak Area

The villages of Togiak and Twin Hills, located about sixty-seven miles west of Dillingham, are the most northwestern settlements in Bristol Bay. Total population for the area in 1970 was more than 450 persons (see Table 1-2). Togiak, which has a population of 388, is the largest Native village in Bristol Bay. Twin Hills, which was first enumerated in the 1970 census, is a small village of sixty-seven persons located about three miles north of Togiak. The population of these communities is 98 percent Eskimo, and the Eskimo culture has a strong influence in the area.[26] Many residents still speak Yupik Eskimo, and they rely very heavily on traditional subsistence pursuits for their livelihood.

The Togiak area has exhibited by far the most rapid population growth of any area in Bristol Bay. The village of Togiak grew from 108 in 1950 to 220 in 1960, an increase of 104 percent. It increased another 74 percent between 1960 and 1970. If the population of Twin Hills is included, the regional population increased by more than 100 percent for the 1960-70 period. This growth rate is due in part to a high rate of natural increase, but it also reflects a substantial amount of migration into the area.

Although it is a relatively large and very rapidly growing village, Togiak is at present able to provide only limited community services. It has no water system.[27] However, electric power is now being supplied by a recently installed Alaska Village Electrification Cooperative (AVEC) facility.

The primary source of income and employment is a cannery located just across the mouth of the Togiak River. This cannery, according to a 1966 Bureau of Indian Affairs (BIA) report, has pro-

---

[26]U.S. Department of the Interior, Bureau of Indian Affairs, *Togiak, Alaska — Village Study* (August 1966) p. 6.

[27]Ibid., p. 7.

vided unusually attractive employment opportunities for the Natives in Togiak, and this has been a major factor contributing to rapid population growth. The same report estimates the average income in Togiak to be over $5,000.[28] However, a 1963 BIA study estimated the average household income to be between $2,000 and $3,000 for the period 1960-62.[29] Nonetheless, it does appear that Togiak fishermen are better off than other Natives in Bristol Bay, with a relatively stable source of income.

Until recently, the only store in Togiak was run by the cannery. In 1970, the village established a cooperative store with financing from the Community Enterprise Development Corporation (CEDC). Within the first two years of operation, the store reduced consumer prices in Togiak by an estimated 25 percent.[30] Supplies are also available from Dillingham, which is about 70 miles east of Togiak. Dillingham is accessible by boat during the summer and by a maintained snow machine trail in the winter.

North Peninsula Villages

There are five small villages in the North Peninsula region— Levelock, Egegik, Pilot Point, Ugashik, and Port Heiden. Levelock is geographically remote from the others, but is included in this group since it is not within Bristol Bay Borough. Between 1960 and 1970, the population in most of these villages showed only a slight increase. In 1970, most of the 421 persons in these villages were Aleuts. Salmon fishing is the primary source of cash income in these communities. Wage income is supplemented by subsistence fishing and hunting and a small amount of trapping.

Egegik: The largest of the villages is Egegik, located forty air

---

[28] Ibid., pp. 2-13.

[29] U.S. Department of the Interior, Bureau of Indian Affairs, *Community Development Survey: Native Village of Togiak, Alaska* (June 1963) p. 5.

[30] CEDC, Contract, p. V-82.

miles south of King Salmon. The village population rose from 86 in 1929 to 150 in 1960, an increase of 74 percent. The population remained constant through 1970 when 153 persons were enumerated. There are three salmon canneries in Egegik, and due to the poor salmon runs in recent years, these are the only ones still operating in this part of Bristol Bay.

Pilot Point: Pilot Point is a predominantly Native village located eighty miles from King Salmon near a salmon cannery which is no longer operating. The village has an air-taxi which serves the Alaska Peninsula. Pilot Point's population has remained relatively constant in the past twenty years with counts of sixty-seven in 1950, sixty-one in 1960, and sixty-eight in 1970.

Ugashik: Ugashik, situated about seven miles from Pilot Point, is the smallest village in the North Peninsula area. A cannery once operated in the community, but is closed now. The population of Ugashik declined steadily from eighty-four in 1929 to thirty-six in 1960. In 1970 the population fell to twenty-two and was not included in the published census reports as the population was less than twenty-five.

Port Heiden: Port Heiden, located about 150 air miles from King Salmon, is the most remote community in Bristol Bay. During the summer, most of the residents move to the Pilot Point area to fish for salmon. They also do some trapping and seal hunting.[31] Port Heiden was first enumerated by the census in 1960 as a community of seventy-four persons. In 1970, the population increased about 9 percent to a total of eighty-one persons. Included in this village population total, there are nine personnel based at a U.S. Air Force radar station about seven miles from the town.[32] Reeve Aleutian Airways maintains a small station at the Port Heiden Airport,[33] midway between the town and the Air Force Station.

---

[31] U.S. Department of the Interior, Bureau of Indian Affairs, *Port Heiden, Alaska — Village Study* (1966) pp. 4-5.

[32] Port Heiden Community Survey by Itinerant Public Health Nurse, 1969.

[33] USDI, *Port Heiden Study*, p. 5.

Historical Patterns of Population Change

Archeological and ethnohistorical evidence indicates that there were about 2,400 aboriginal inhabitants in Bristol Bay prior to white contact (see Figure 2-1). Over 60 percent of this population was centered in the vicinity of the Nushagak-Togiak Bay and river system. About 400 persons were located in the vicinity of Iliamna Lake, and another 500 inhabited the Kvichak Bay—North Peninsula area. Except for a small number of Tanaina Athabascans on the eastern end of Lake Iliamna, all of Bristol Bay's aboriginal inhabitants were Yupik (Southern) Eskimos.[1]

In 1778, English Captain James Cook visited Bristol Bay and wrote a description of the area. However, it was not until 1818 that the first white settlers, Russians, built trading posts in the region at Iliamna and Nushagak Bay.[2]

White contact seemed to cause no massive reduction in the Native population of the Bristol Bay area, although in other parts of Alaska Native populations were often decimated by conflict and disease in the early years after white contact. There were some scattered reports of epidemics in Bristol Bay, and a few villages were plundered by the Russians, but evidently neither of these had drastic effects on the Native populations, probably because white-Native interaction was minimal.

---

[1] Oswalt, *Alaskan Eskimos*, Map 4.

[2] Margaret Lentis, ed., *Ethnohistory in Southwestern Alaska and the Southern Yukon* (Lexington, Kentucky: University Press of Kentucky, 1970) p. 82.

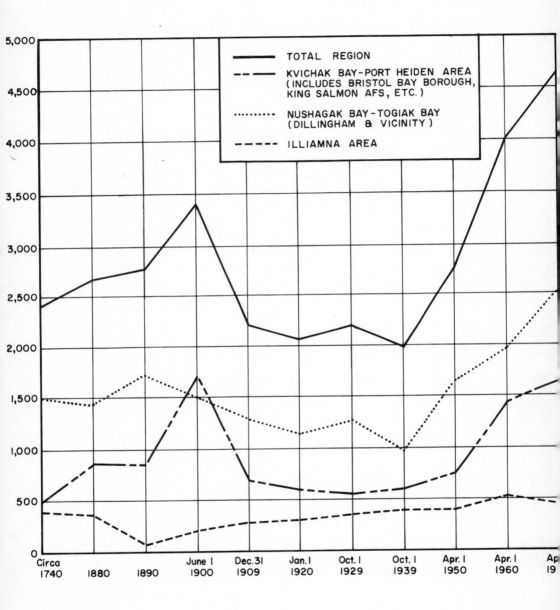

Figure 2-1: Regional Distribution of Population, Bristol Bay, 1740-1940

While Natives in other regions of Alaska often lived in large permanent coastal settlements, much of the Native population in the Bristol Bay area lived inland in widely dispersed small villages and ventured down the rivers for only a few weeks each year to harvest the salmon runs or to trade furs.

Russian interest in Bristol Bay centered primarily on the fur trade, and their sphere of influence was generally limited to Natives living in the immediate area. Around 1830, Russian Orthodox missionaries began working to convert the Natives to Christianity. This influence, however, was limited because of the scattered and mobile Native populations.

By 1880, Bristol Bay's estimated population was about 2,700, an increase of only 12 percent over the estimated pre-contact population. Thus, from aboriginal times to the beginning of the commercial exploitation of Bristol Bay's salmon resources, there were few changes in the area's population.[3]

The establishment of the commercial fishing and salmon canning industries in Bristol Bay in the 1880's brought about much more extensive contact between whites and the Native-populations.[4] The increased interaction exposed the Natives to diseases for which they had no natural immunity, and this resulted in several epidemics in the region.

The population of Bristol Bay reached a peak around the turn of the century and then declined slowly for the next four decades. By 1939, the population had fallen more than 25 percent below the level observed in 1890.

Primarily as a result of World War II military activity, the Bristol Bay region exhibited a nearly 40-percent population increase between 1939 and 1950. One direct cause of the growth was the establishment of Naknek Army Air Force Base (later renamed King

---

[3] Van Stone, *Eskimos*, pp. 22-24.

[4] Ibid., p. 63.

Salmon) and other defense sites. By 1950, the population in the Kvichak Bay-North Peninsula area was 752, an increase of 25 percent over the 1939 level. Most of the increase, however, was in the Togiak-Nushagak area. Shortly before the war there were less than 1,000 persons in the area and by 1950 there were 1,636.

By 1960, Bristol Bay's population exceeded 4,000 persons, an increase of more than 45 percent over the preceding decade. Most of this growth was concentrated in the Kvichak Bay area, which exhibited a 90-percent population gain. This was largely due to the expansion and modernization of the facilities at the King Salmon Air Force Base and airport.

Recent Population Patterns

The rate of population growth in Bristol Bay dropped sharply between 1960 and 1970. The increase for the decade was just 15 percent, or an average annual increase of about 1.4 percent. That rate is clearly lower than the rate of natural increase due to births and deaths and thus implies that people were migrating from the Bristol Bay region during the decade. As shown in Table 2-1, a part of the population slowdown is attributable to the reduction in military personnel stationed in the area. The civilian population increased by 20 percent while the military personnel were being reduced by 18 percent.

Roughly two-thirds of the residents of Bristol Bay are nonwhites (see Table 2-1). In 1970, over 97 percent of the nonwhites were Natives (Indians, Aleuts, and Eskimos).[5] The Native population in Bristol Bay gained less than 17 percent between 1960 and 1970, for an average annual increase of 1.6 percent, a growth rate far below the rate of natural increase. This would seem to indicate significant amounts of Native migration out of the Bristol Bay region. The figures in Table 2-2, although only approximations, provide estimates of natural increase and migration as the sources of population growth. The estimated net increase in civilian Native population was

---

[5]Throughout the remainder of this report the term "Native" will be used synonymously with "nonwhite."

Table 2-1
POPULATION GROWTH
BRISTOL BAY 1960-70

	1960 Census			1970 Census			% Change of Total 1960-1970
	Male	Female	Total	Male	Female	Total	
Total Population	2,404	1,620	4,024	2,632	2,000	4,632	15.1
Civilian	1,868	1,620	3,488	2,197	1,996	4,193	20.2
Military Personnel	536	–	536	435	4	439	–18.1
White	1,039	384	1,423	1,042	551	1,593	11.9
Nonwhite	1,365	1,236	2,601	1,570	1,449	3,039	16.8
Negro	26	1	27	32	4	36	33.3
Indian	115	118	233	144	148	292	16.6[b]
Aleut	–	–	–	494	472	966	
Eskimo	–	–	–	880	811	1,691	
Other	1,244[a]	1,117[a]	2,341[a]	40	14	54	

[a] In 1960 Census, Aleut and Eskimo are lumped in the "other" category.
[b] Represents approximate percentage change in the Native population.

2-5

Table 2-2
COMPONENTS OF POPULATION CHANGE
BRISTOL BAY   1960-70

	All Races			White			Nonwhite		
	1960	1970	Change 1960-70	1960	1970	Change 1960-70	1960	1970	Change 1960-70
Population	4024	4632	608	1423	1593	170	2601	3039	438
Military Personnel	536	439	-97	482	395	-87	54	44	-10
Civilian Population	3488	4193	705	945	1198	253	2547	2995	448
Births	157	102	1263	29	16	179	128	86	1082
Deaths	26	29	316	3	5	89	23	22	223
Natural Increase	131	73	947	26	11	90	105	64	859
Rate of Natural Increase (total population)	3.26%	1.58%	2.19%	1.83%	0.69%	0.60%	4.04%	2.11%	3.05%
Rate of Natural Increase (civilian population)	3.76%	1.74%	2.46%	2.75%	0.92%	0.84%	4.12%	2.13%	3.10%
Migration	--	--	-339	--	--	80	--	--	-421
Civilian Migration	--	--	-242	--	--	163	--	--	-411

Source: U.S. Department of Commerce, Bureau of the Census, 1960 Census, Alaska, Tables 15 and 28; Babb, "Age and Sex Characteristics of Alaska's Population," Table 5; U.S. Department of Commerce, Bureau of the Census, 1970 Census, Alaska, Table 121.

448 persons, while the natural increase was 859 persons. Thus, there was a net out-migration of more than 400 persons. In contrast, two-thirds of the growth in the civilian white population was due to net migration into the area. The total white population increased by 170 persons despite a reduction in military personnel and a very low rate of natural increase.

Table 2-2 also contains estimates of the rates of natural increase for 1960, 1970, and average rates over the decade. For all population groups shown, there is an extremely sharp drop in the rate of natural increase between 1960 and 1970. This is due to the reduction in the birthrate during that period.[6] This phenomenon occurred throughout the country and is generally attributed to several factors. There were improvements in birth control methods, programs to provide information on family planning, and a general change in social attitudes regarding family planning. In the Bristol Bay region, the Native rate of natural increase was cut nearly in half, falling from 4 percent in 1960 to 2 percent in 1970. Further evidence confirming the drop in birthrates is provided by the fertility ratios in Figure 2-2.[7] By including data for Alaska and the U.S., the figure shows that the decline in the birthrate was indeed widespread. Despite the recent decline, the Bristol Bay fertility ratios for both whites and nonwhites remain high relative to the U.S. and Alaska averages. Also, the fertility ratio for nonwhites in Bristol Bay remains much higher than the ratio for whites.

As shown in Table 2-3, Bristol Bay has only two modest concentrations of population, Dillingham and Bristol Bay Borough. Together these two areas contain about 40 percent of the civilian population of the Bristol Bay region. It is difficult to figure

---

[6] George W. Rogers, *Alaska Native Population Trends and Vital Statistics, 1950-1985*, ISEGR Research Note (Fairbanks: University of Alaska, Institute of Social, Economic and Government Research, November 1971.) p. 10.

[7] For a discussion of fertility ratios, see George W. Rogers and Richard Cooley, *Alaska's Population and Economy, Volume 1 Analysis*, Economic Series Publication No. 1., Vol. 1 (Fairbanks: University of Alaska, Institute of Social, Economic and Government Research, 1963.) pp. 104-107.

Table 2-3
POPULATION OF TOWNS AND VILLAGES,
BRISTOL BAY, 1929-1970

	1929	1939	1950	1960	1970	% change 1950–1960	% change 1960-1970
TOTAL: BRISTOL BAY	**2,198**	**1,992**	**2,756**	**4,024**	**4,632**	**46.0**	**15.1**
TOGIAK–NUSHAGAK	**1,289**	**993**	**1,636**	**1,987**	**2,510**	21.5	26.3
Unspecified Places	891	424	157	434	101	–	–
Nushagak Bay Region							
Aleknagik	–	78	153	231	219	51.0	-5.2
Clarks Point	25	22	128	138	95	7.8	-31.2
Dillingham	85	278	577	424	914	-26.5	NA[a]
Ekuk	–	–	–	40	51	–	27.5
Kanakanak	177	113	54	–	–	–	–
Manakotak	–	–	120	149	214	24.2	43.6
Tuklung	–	–	30	–	–	–	–
Nushagak River Region							
Ekwok	40	68	131	106	103	-19.1	-2.8
Koliganek	–	–	90	100	142	11.1	42.0
New Stuyahok	–	–	88	145	216	64.8	49.0
Portage Creek[b]					60[b]		
Togiak Bay Region							
Togiak	71	10	108	220	388	103.7	76.4
Twin Hills	–	–	–	–	67	–	–

(continued on next page)

Table 2-3 (continued)

	358	399	368	611	554	66.0	-9.3
ILIAMNA							
Unspecified Places	234	232	42	152	13	—	—
Iliamna Lake Region							
Igiugig					36	—	—
Iliamna	100	30	44	47	58	6.8	23.4
Kakhonak			39	57	88	46.2	54.4
Newhalen		55	48	63	88	31.3	39.7
Nondalton	24	82	103	205	184	99.0	-10.2
Pedro Bay			44	53	65	20.5	22.6
Pile Bay			48	—	—	—	—
Port Alsworth			—	34	22	—	-35.3
KVICHAK–ALASKA PENINSULA	**551**	**600**	**752**	**1,426**	**1,568**	**89.6**	**10.0**
Unspecified Places	208	154	268	77	70	—	—
Bristol Bay Borough							
King Salmon			—	227	202	—	-11.0
King Salmon A.F.B.			—	322	403	—	25.2
Naknek	173	152	174	249	318	43.1	27.7
South Naknek			—	142	154	—	8.5
Alaska Peninsula Region							
Egegik	86	125	119	150	153	26.1	2.0
Levelock		—	76	88	98	15.8	11.4
Pilot Point		114	67	61	68	-9.0	11.5
Port Heiden			—	74	81	—	9.5
Ugashik	84	55	48	36	21	-25.0	-41.7

Sources: U.S. Department of Commerce, Bureau of the Census, *1950 Census, Alaska*, Tables 4 and 5; *1960 Census, Alaska*, Table 8; *1960 Census, Alaska*, enumeration worksheets; *1970 Census, Alaska*, Table 10; *1970 Census, Alaska*, special computer runs.

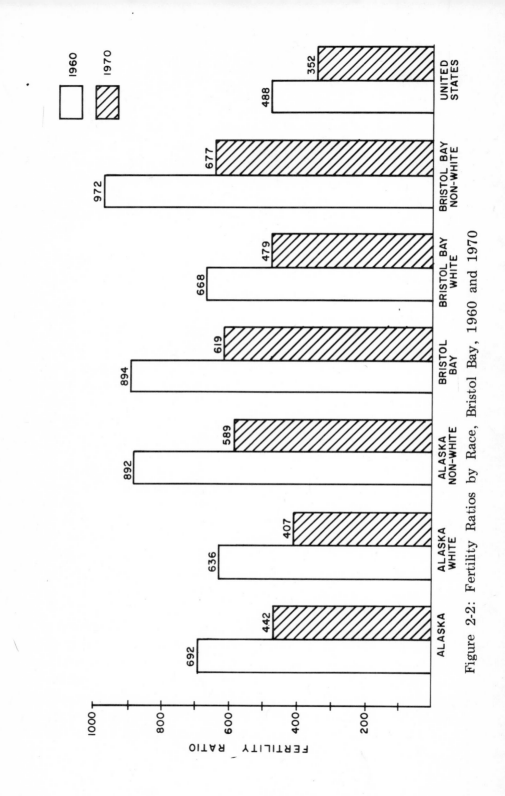

Figure 2-2: Fertility Ratios by Race, Bristol Bay, 1960 and 1970

population changes over time for either of these areas because neither Dillingham nor the Bristol Bay Borough were incorporated until after the 1960 census. However, if the 1960 population of the Dillingham area is estimated to have been 800,[8] then the growth for the area during the decade was 14 percent. The average growth of the towns within Bristol Bay Borough that were enumerated in the 1960 census was 15 percent.

The rest of Bristol Bay's population is dispersed widely over the nineteen communities reported in the 1970 census and several smaller villages not reported in the census.

Perhaps the most striking feature of the population change in Bristol Bay is the extremely rapid growth in the Eskimo communities of Koliganek, Manokotak, Kakhonak, New Stuyahok, Togiak, and Twin Hills. The cumulative population of these villages went from about 640 persons in 1960 to more than 1,100 in 1970, an increase of 66 percent. Virtually the entire population of the villages is Eskimo (see Table 2-4), and the influence of the Eskimo culture is very strong. An Eskimo dialect is generally spoken, with English used only as necessary. Also, because these fast-growing villages are relatively remote from any urban centers, the pattern of population change among the Bristol Bay Eskimos might almost be described as a process of "de-urbanization." It is clear that a substantial part of the very rapid growth in the Eskimo communities must be due to migration either from other villages or from outside the region. Unfortunately, the 1960 data do not provide separate estimates for the Eskimo population, so the precise changes cannot be traced.

In 1970, Eskimos in Bristol Bay numbered 1,691 persons and accounted for about 33 percent of the population (see Table 2-4). Nearly two-thirds of the Eskimo population (about 1,100 persons) is located in the six villages discussed above. Whites, which number 1,593, make up 34 percent of the population and are concentrated largely in the urbanized areas of Dillingham or Bristol Bay Borough. Aleuts, which number 966 persons, constitute 20 percent of the

---

[8]ASHA. *Dillingham Comprehensive Plan*, p. 33.

Table 2-4
COMMUNITY POPULATION BY RACE AND SEX
BRISTOL BAY 1970

PLACE	All Races			White			Negro		
	M	F	T	M	F	T	M	F	T
Bristol Bay Borough[a]	788	359	1,147	688	254	922	30	1	31
King Salmon	98	104	202	95	95	190	0	0	0
Naknek	164	154	318	129	103	232	0	1	1
South Naknek	84	70	154	43	26	69	0	0	0
King Salmon A.F.B.	403	0	403	364	0	364	30	0	30
Bristol Bay Division[a]	1,844	1,641	3,485	374	297	671	2	3	5
Aleknagik	120	99	219	27	32	59	0	0	0
Clarks Point	47	48	95	10	10	20	0	0	0
Dillingham	465	449	914	167	158	325	0	1	1
Egegik	81	72	153	43	32	75	1	1	2
Ekuk	28	23	51	0	0	0	1	0	1
Ekwok	54	49	103	4	4	8	0	0	0
Igiugig	20	16	36	1	1	2	0	0	0
Iliamna	34	24	58	21	14	35	0	0	0
Kakhonak	43	45	88	9	6	15	0	0	0
Koliganek	71	71	142	5	3	8	0	0	0
Levelock	55	43	98	11	5	16	0	0	0
Manokotak	107	107	214	3	6	9	0	0	0
Newhalen	54	34	88	3	2	5	0	0	0
New Stuyahok	118	98	216	6	2	8	0	0	0
Nondalton	92	92	184	2	0	2	0	0	0
Pedro Bay	35	30	65	6	2	8	0	1	1
Pilot Point	40	28	68	6	4	10	0	0	0
Port Heiden	50	31	81	16	5	21	0	0	0
Togiak	206	182	388	2	4	6	0	0	0
Twin Hills	35	32	67	1	0	1	0	0	0
TOTAL — BRISTOL BAY	2,632	2,000	4,632	1,042	551	1,593	32	4	64

[a]Totals include unspecified places

Sources: Ron Evans and Peggy Raybeck, "Age and Race by Sex Characteristics of Alaska's Village Population," Vol. 10 No. 2, Fairbanks: Institute of Social, Economic and Government Research, 1973; U.S. Department of Commerce, Bureau of the Census, 1970 Census Alaska, special computer runs.

Table 2-4 (continued from facing page)

Indian			Aleut			Eskimo			Other		
M	F	T	M	F	T	M	F	T	M	F	T
8	12	20	59	72	131	16	19	35	7	1	8
1	3	4	1	6	7	1	0	1	0	0	0
6	9	15	22	27	49	5	13	18	0	1	1
0	0	0	36	39	75	5	5	10	0	0	0
1	0	1	0	0	0	3	0	3	5	0	5
132	133	272	435	400	835	864	792	1,656	33	13	46
0	0	0	3	0	3	89	64	153	1	3	4
0	0	0	18	23	41	11	14	25	8	1	9
5	8	13	191	195	386	96	87	183	6	0	6
0	0	0	34	38	72	3	1	4	0	0	0
0	0	0	2	2	4	17	17	34	8	4	12
0	0	0	16	16	32	33	29	62	1	0	1
1	0	1	15	10	25	3	5	8	0	0	0
11	7	18	1	1	2	1	2	3	0	0	0
0	0	0	0	0	0	32	35	67	2	4	6
0	0	0	0	0	0	66	68	134	0	0	0
0	0	0	36	29	65	8	9	17	0	0	0
0	0	0	0	0	0	104	101	205	0	0	0
3	0	3	48	32	80	0	0	0	0	0	0
0	0	0	0	0	0	112	96	208	0	0	0
90	92	182	0	0	0	0	0	0	0	0	0
21	26	47	1	1	2	2	0	2	5	0	5
0	0	0	31	23	54	3	1	4	0	0	0
1	0	1	33	26	59	0	0	0	0	0	0
0	0	0	0	0	0	205	177	382	0	0	0
0	0	0	0	0	0	34	32	66	0	0	0
144	148	292	494	472	966	880	811	1,691	40	14	54

population of Bristol Bay. A majority of Bristol Bay's Aleuts, 386, live in Dillingham and comprise the largest ethnic group in the community. The Indian population in Bristol Bay is 292 persons, almost all of which are concentrated in the Eastern Iliamna area, particularly Nondalton and Pedro Bay.

In general then, the population of Bristol Bay is characterized by a wide diversity of racial and cultural backgrounds, with no single group predominating. However, in some important instances the ethnic groups have tended to concentrate in specific communities rather than being dispersed throughout the region. Examples of this are the purely Eskimo or Indian villages. The most outstanding aspect of population change in recent years is the extremely rapid growth of the Eskimo communities. There has been a major population shift into these communities during the past decade.

Education

In the nineteenth century, Russian Orthodox and Moravian missionaries attempted to initiate educational programs among the Natives of Bristol Bay, but their sporadic efforts had little lasting effect. After Alaska was purchased by the U.S., a vast majority of the population continued to receive little or no education until after World War II. Van Stone related the following illustration:

> During the summer of 1908 an official of the Bureau of Education made his annual inspection of the federally supported schools and visited the Nushagak Bay region to inspect two schools at Carmel and Dillingham. However, he broadened the scope of his inquiry in order to ascertain the educational needs of the people. . . . In talking with people in unspecified places in the area, he was shocked to discover that they had no knowledge of the United States Government and believed themselves still under the rule of Russia. . .his comments suggest that in spite of canneries, missionaries, and other agents of contact, culture change in the Nushagak River region was progressing very slowly.[9]

By the time of statehood, there were about 700 students

---

[9]Van Stone, *Eskimos*, pp. 97 and 99.

enrolled in Bristol Bay schools. Within the next few years and with the completion of a new high school in Dillingham, the enrollment approached 1,000 students. Between 1960-61 and 1970-71, total school enrollment in Bristol Bay rose from 919 to 1,395, an increase of about 52 percent (see Table 2-5 and Figure 2-3). Since 1970-71 the enrollment has remained constant at approximately 1,400 students. The leveling off in school enrollments is attributable to the decline in the birthrate and to the out-migration of families with school-age children.

Elementary school enrollments have declined from a peak of 1,156 students in 1968-69 to 1,042 students in 1972-73, a drop of 10 percent in four years. About one-third of the elementary school students attended district schools in Dillingham and the Bristol Bay Borough. In both areas, Native students constitute the majority—about 60 percent in the Bristol Bay Borough and 80 percent at Dillingham elementary school. In rural areas, the state operates elementary schools in nineteen villages (see Table 2-6). These rural schools vary in size from ninety-three students at Togiak to seven at Pedro Bay. The average village school enrollment is thirty-five students. Of 678 village elementary students enrolled in Bristol Bay in 1972-73, all but twenty-two were Natives.

In contrast to the elementary school trend, high school enrollments rose steadily from about sixty students in 1960-61 to 280 in 1970-71, a five-fold increase for the decade. This trend has continued with a 1972-73 high school enrollment of 349, an increase of 25 percent in just two years. However, the decline in elementary school enrollment indicates that there will also be a leveling off in the number of high school students within a few years.

Dillingham and the Bristol Bay Borough offer the only complete high school programs in Bristol Bay, though schools at Togiak, Igiugig, and Nondalton offer limited secondary curriculums. The lack of high school programs in the villages is due to low population and the scattered distribution of settlements. Some village students attend Bureau of Indian Affairs high schools in Alaska or other states, but most go to Dillingham High School and

Table 2-5
TOTAL SCHOOL ENROLLMENT
BRISTOL BAY 1958–1959 to 1971-1972

Year	Elementary School				High School				Total	% Increase from previous year
	White	Native	Other	Subtotal	White	Native	Other	Subtotal		
1958-59	96	628	0	724	0	0	0	0	724	—
1959-60	91	720	14	825	5	53	—	58	883	22
1960-61	131	742	0	873	0	46	0	46	919	4
1961-62	NA	NA	NA	NA	NA	NA	NA	NA	NA	NA
1962-63	116	858	4	978	7	65	0	72	1050	NA
1963-64	129	900	2	1031	22	73	0	95	1126	7
1964-65	93	955	0	1048	18	87	0	105	1153	3
1965-66	123	953	0	1076	18	94	0	112	1188	3
1966-67	155	942	—	1097	16	115	0	131	1228	4
1967-68	160	977	0	1137	22	136	0	158	1295	5
1968-69	207	949	0	1156	25	127	0	152	1308	1
1969-70	171	943	0	1114	44	153	0	197	1311	0.2
1970-71	137	979	0	1116	61	218	0	279	1395	6
1971-72	150	968	0	1118	66	224	0	290	1408	1
1972-73	133	909	0	1039	83	266	0	349	1391	-1

Sources: Sullivan and Rose, *Alaska School Enrollments*, page 27, Alaska Department of Education.

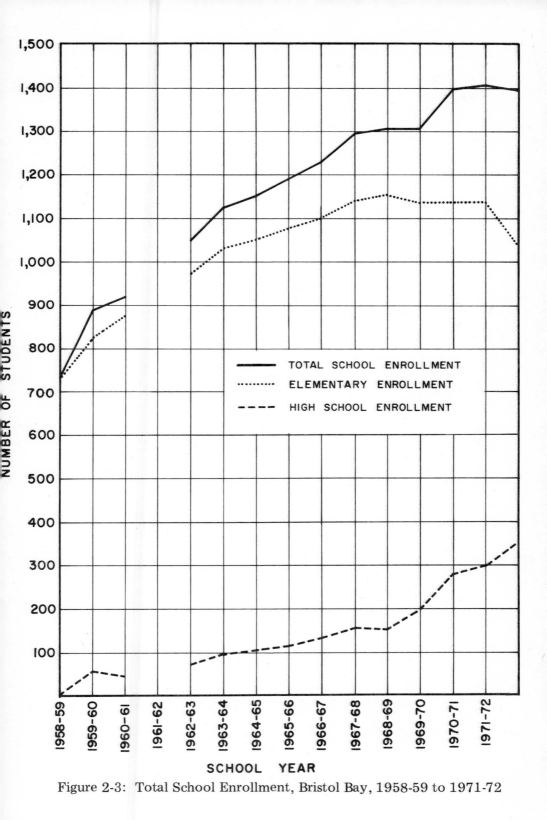

Figure 2-3: Total School Enrollment, Bristol Bay, 1958-59 to 1971-72

Table 2-6
SCHOOL ENROLLMENTS BY COMMUNITY
BRISTOL BAY 1972-1973

	Elementary School			High School			Total
	White	Native	Subtotal	White	Native	Subtotal	
District Schools							
Bristol Bay	56	87	143	51	85	136	279
Dillingham	43	161	204	30	128	158	362
Subtotals	99	248	347	81	213	294	641
Rural Schools							
Aleknagik	7	23	30				30
Clarks Point		22	22				22
Egegik	1	33	34				34
Ekuk		12	12				12
Ekwok		28	28				28
Igiugig	3	11	14				14
Kakhanak		28	28				28
Koliganek		43	43				43
Levelock		28	28				28
Manokotak	2	82	84				84
Newhalen	5	34	39				39
New Stuyahok		75	75				75
Nondalton	2	63	65	2	7	9	74
North Aleknagik		14	14			46	14
Pedro Bay		7	7				7

(continued on next page)

Table 2-6 (continued)

Pilot Point	2	16	18				18
Port Heiden		22	22				22
Togiak		93	93		46	46	139
Twin Hills		25	25				25
Subtotals	22	659	678	2	53	55	736
Private and Denominational Schools							
Dillingham SDA	12	2	14				14
TOTALS	133	909	1,042	83	266	349	1,388

Source: Alaska Department of Education.

2-19

live with local families under the state boarding home program.[10]

Although the availability of education has increased tremendously in the past twenty years, the traditional school program has often failed to meet the needs of many students, particularly Natives. A staff member of the Alaska Department of Education explained the situation at Dillingham High School:

> ...isolation, combined with the fact that about 90 percent of the villagers have some degree of Alaska Eskimo or Aleut background, created educational needs that the traditional school program was not meeting. Because of language and cultural barriers, the typical Native students were often three years behind national norms in reading and composition skills by the time they entered the ninth grade. Though there were indications that they were just as intelligent as the white students, they had lost confidence in their ability to compete with them academically. As a consequence, many Native students dropped out before completing high school, and very few ever attempted college. Indeed, no more than five students out of a class of 30 had ever gone to college and survived the first year.[11]

In an innovative attempt to broaden the experiences and increase the potential of Bristol Bay students, Dillingham High School initiated a Japan Study Program in 1970-71. The program was financed primarily through state and federal funds. The Japan study program, which included both Native and white students, began with intensive instruction in Japanese language and culture. Following this training, twenty-eight students traveled in Japan and took courses from teachers in the group. Upon their return to Alaska some students completed their high school requirements by taking courses at the University of Alaska. During the 1971-72 school year, the Japan study-travel program was expanded to forty-nine students—eighteen from Bristol Bay and the remainder from other rural Alaska communities. In 1972-73, students from Bristol Bay

---

[10]Ronald Klemm, regional coordinator for State-Operated Schools, personal communication, December 1973.

[11]Russell Jones, "On Equal Footing" *Today's Education,* March 1972.

were among 140 students who participated in study-travel programs to Japan and Spain.

Although the study-travel programs have been termed a success by the students who participated and persons evaluating the programs, they are extremely expensive to operate. In addition, it is difficult to measure the effect of these programs on the students and their particular home communities. It would seem that students who took part in the programs broadened their educational goals and occupational expectations. There was also an increase in the number of students who succeeded in college work. For example, thirty-six students graduated from Dillingham High School in 1971, and a year later, twenty-one of these were enrolled in college programs.[12]

Educational Attainment

Alaska has historically had a relatively high educational attainment level.[13] This trend continued in 1970 as the average number of school years completed by both males and females in Alaska were higher than for the total U.S. (see Table 2-7). However, the lack of educational opportunities in Bristol Bay until the recent period is reflected in much lower-than-average education levels.

One measure of educational attainment is the percentage of high school graduates in the over-twenty-five population. Bristol Bay's figures of 45.8 percent for males and 34.2 percent for females are far below state averages of 66.3 percent for males and 67.1 percent for females. When these statistics are separated by race, it is apparent that the low percentage of high school graduates is only characteristic of the Native population. More than 75 percent of Bristol Bay whites are high school graduates, which is approximately

---

[12]Diana Holzmeuller, Assistant Educational Program Developer, Center for Northern Educational Research, University of Alaska, Fairbanks, personal communication, December 1973.

[13]Rogers and Cooley, *Alaska's Population and Economy*, p. 86.

Table 2-7
EDUCATIONAL ATTAINMENT
BRISTOL BAY 1970

Years of School Completed	Bristol Bay					
	Total		White		Nonwhite	
	Number	Percent	Number	Percent	Number	Percent
Males, 24 yrs. old and over	1,083	100.0	520	100.0	563	100.0
No school years completed	129	11.9	0	-	129	22.9
Elementary: 1-4 years	192	17.7	13	2.5	179	31.8
5-6 years	55	5.1	0	-	55	9.8
7 years	73	6.7	34	6.5	39	6.9
8 years	80	7.4	28	5.4	52	9.2
High School: 1-3 years	58	5.4	44	8.5	14	2.5
4 years	281	25.9	218	41.9	63	11.2
College: 1-3 years	111	10.2	88	16.9	23	4.8
4 years	64	5.9	60	11.5	4	0.7
5 years or more	40	3.7	35	6.7	5	0.9
High School Graduates	457	45.8	401	77.1	95	16.9
Females, 25 yrs. old and over	763	100.0	276	100.0	487	100.0
No school years completed	123	16.1	4	1.4	119	24.4
Elementary: 1-4 years	161	21.1	5	1.8	156	32.0
5-6 years	46	6.0	5	1.8	41	8.4
7 years	32	4.2	8	2.9	24	4.9
8 years	69	9.0	21	7.6	48	9.9
High School: 1-3 years	71	9.3	26	9.4	45	9.2
4 years	119	15.6	93	33.7	26	5.3
College: 1-3 years	64	8.4	46	16.6	18	3.7
4 years	46	6.0	42	15.2	4	0.8
5 years or more	32	4.2	26	9.4	6	1.2
High School Graduates	261	34.2	207	75.0	54	11.1
Total, 25 yrs. old and over	1,846	100.0	796	100.0	1,050	100.0
No school years completed	252	13.7	4	0.5	248	23.6
Elementary: 1-4 years	353	19.1	18	2.3	335	31.9
5-6 years	101	5.5	5	0.6	96	9.1
7 years	105	5.7	42	5.2	63	6.0
8 years	149	8.1	49	6.2	100	9.5
High School: 1-3 years	129	7.0	70	8.9	59	5.6
4 years	400	21.7	311	39.1	89	8.5
College: 1-3 years	175	9.5	134	16.8	41	3.9
4 years	110	6.0	102	12.8	8	0.8
5 years or more	72	3.9	61	7.7	11	1.0
High School Graduates	757	41.0	608	76.4	149	14.2

Sources: U.S. Department of Commerce, Bureau of the Census, *1970 Census*, Alaska, special computer runs; and *1970 Census*, United States Summary, Table 88.

Table 2-7 (continued from previous page)

Alaska						U.S.	
Total		White		Nonwhite		Total	
Number	Percent	Number	Percent	Number	Percent	Number	Percent
73,963	100.0	61,189	100.0	12,774	100.0	51,869,770	100.0
1,774	2.4	267	0.4	1,507	11.8	852,851	1.6
2,612	3.5	435	0.7	2,177	17.0	2,299,323	4.4
2,180	2.9	656	1.2	1,524	11.9	3,082,912	5.9
1,883	2.5	1,024	1.7	859	6.7	2,392,567	4.6
5,653	7.6	4,378	7.2	1,275	10.0	6,708,041	12.9
10,858	14.9	9,116	14.9	1,742	13.6	9,633,537	18.6
26,684	36.1	24,258	39.6	2,426	19.0	14,365,218	27.7
10,829	14.6	9,994	16.3	835	6.5	5,526,759	10.7
5,612	7.6	5,359	8.8	253	2.0	3,518,159	6.8
5,878	7.9	5,702	9.3	176	1.4	3,490,403	6.7
	66.3	45,313	74.1	12,774	28.9		51.9
60,985	100.0	49,717	100.0	11,268	100.0	58,029,589	100.0
1,565	2.6	177	0.3	1,388	12.3	914,902	1.6
2,009	3.3	197	0.4	1,812	16.1	1,972,238	3.4
1,944	3.2	456	0.9	1,488	13.2	3,134,180	5.4
1,248	2.0	486	1.0	762	6.8	2,423,053	4.2
3,974	6.5	2,570	5.2	1,404	12.5	7,307,323	12.6
9,294	15.2	7,676	15.4	1,618	14.4	11,652,385	20.1
24,136	39.6	22,285	44.8	1,851	16.4	19,792,833	34.1
9,223	15.1	8,604	17.3	619	5.5	6,123,971	10.6
4,872	8.0	4,622	9.3	250	2.2	3,139,445	5.4
2,720	4.5	2,644	5.3	76	0.7	1,569,259	2.7
	67.1	38,115	76.7	11,268	24.8		52.8
134,948	100.0	110,906	100.0	24,042	100.0	109,899,359	100.0
3,339	2.5	444	0.4	2,895	12.0	1,767,753	1.6
4,621	3.4	632	0.6	3,989	16.6	4,271,561	3.9
4,124	3.1	1,112	1.0	3,012	12.5	6,217,092	5.7
3,131	2.3	1,510	1.4	1,621	6.7	4,815,620	4.4
9,627	7.1	6,948	6.3	2,679	11.1	14,015,364	12.6
20,152	14.9	16,792	15.1	3,360	14.0	21,285,922	19.4
50,820	37.6	46,543	42.0	4,277	17.8	34,158,051	31.1
20,052	14.9	18,598	16.8	1,454	6.0	11,650,730	10.6
10,484	7.8	9,981	9.0	503	2.1	6,657,604	6.1
8,598	6.4	8,346	7.5	252	1.0	5,059	4.6
	66.6		75.3		26.9		52.4

the statewide average for whites. However, less than 15 percent of the Natives are high school graduates.

At the other end of the scale, Alaska also tends to have a relatively large proportion of persons over twenty-five who have no education at all. In the U.S., only 1.6 percent of the population has no education, while the Alaska average is 2.5 percent. In Bristol Bay, the proportion of the over-twenty-five population with no education is 11.9 percent for males and 16.1 for females. Again this indication of educational deficiency is characteristic only of the Native population. Less than 1 percent of the white, over-twenty-five population have no education. But nearly 24 percent of the Natives have no education, a figure double the state average.

CHAPTER 3
LABOR FORCE
AND EMPLOYMENT

Labor Force

The size of the labor force in any region is determined both by the characteristics of the local population and by the availability of employment opportunities. In the long run, there has to be a close relationship between the size of the population and the size of the labor force. However, this relationship is not necessarily constant over time, nor is it the same for all regions. For instance, participation rates can vary widely within a population seeking employment. One of the key factors determining the participation rate is the availability of employment. When jobs are easy to find, more people decide to seek employment, thus causing an increase in the participation rate and in the labor force.

In the Bristol Bay region, both the size of the local population and the employment opportunities are subject to large fluctuations due to outside forces. This is most evident in the fishing and fish processing industry which exhibits extreme variation seasonally and from one year to another because of weather conditions and cycles in the fish populations. It is therefore not surprising to find that the work force in Bristol Bay, while generally increasing, varies considerably over the long-run growth trend (See Figure 3-1). In Bristol Bay, the average civilian work force in 1971-72 was 30 percent larger than the average work force in 1961-62.

Table 3-1 shows how the participation and unemployment rates in the Bristol Bay region compare to the state averages. Participation rates in Bristol Bay are extremely low for both men and women. The male participation rate in Bristol Bay is 49 percent, compared to 79

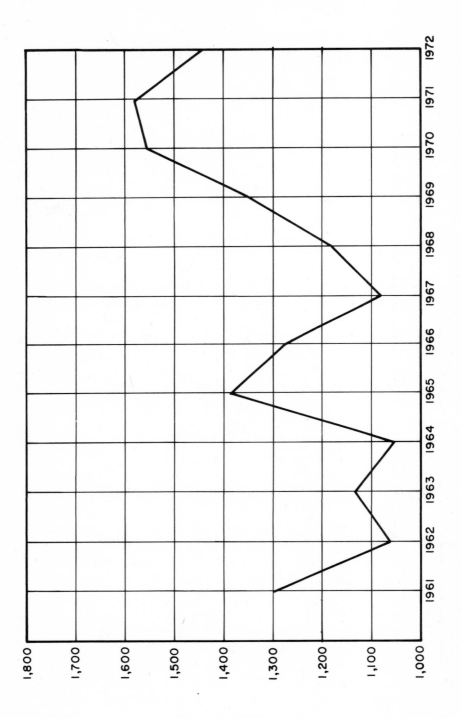

Figure 3-1: Work Force in Bristol Bay Area, 1961-72

Table 3-1
LABOR FORCE AND EMPLOYMENT
BRISTOL BAY 1970

	Bristol Bay Borough	Bristol Bay Division	Bristol Bay Total	Alaska
Total Civilian Population, 16 years old and over	37.0	1,830.0	2,201.0	159,702.0
Civilian labor force	224.0	658.0	882.0	98,296.0
Percent of total (participation rate)	60.4	36.0	40.1	61.5
Employed	165.0	584.0	749.0	89,236.0
Unemployed	59.0	74.0	133.0	9,060.0
Percent of civilian labor force	26.3	11.2	15.1	9.2
Male, 16 years old and over, civilian	205.0	954.0	1,159.0	76,547.0
Civilian labor force	170.0	399.0	569.0	60,293.0
Percent of total (participation rate)	82.9	41.8	49.1	78.8
Employed	111.0	333.0	444.0	54,114.0
Unemployed	59.0	66.0	125.0	6,179.0
Percent of civilian labor force	34.7	16.5	22.0	10.2
Female, 16 years old and over, civilian	166.0	876.0	1,042.0	83,155.0
Civilian labor force	54.0	259.0	313.0	38,003.0
Percent of total (participation rate)	32.5	29.6	30.0	45.7
Employed	54.0	251.0	305.0	35,122.0
Unemployed	0	8.0	8.0	2,881.0
Percent of civilian labor force	0	3.1	2.6	7.6

Source: U.S. Department of Commerce, Bureau of the Census, *1970 Census*, Alaska, Tables 53 and 121.

percent for the state, and the female participation rate is only 30 percent, compared to 46 percent for the state. At the same time, the average unemployment rate is 15 percent, much higher than the rest of the state. A high unemployment rate accompanied by a low participation rate is precisely what would be expected. The lack of employment opportunities has caused people to drop out of the labor force. This picture is also consistent with the migration patterns discussed in Chapter 2. The lack of employment opportunities contributes to the observed migration from the Bristol Bay region.[1]

Seasonal Variation in Employment

Employment in Bristol Bay has been dominated by the pronounced seasonal fluctuations in the fishing industry. Figures 3-2 and 3-3 show the average annual employment and the monthly variations around the average. The graphs illustrate how closely the seasonal movements in the labor force, due to changes in participation rates and an influx of nonresidents, match the movements in employment. During the winter, when jobs are not available, the nonresidents leave and many of the residents simply drop out of the labor force. This process is clearly illustrated in Figure 3-3 by the enormous increase in the labor force during the summer. Furthermore, the increase shown is a significant underestimate of total expansion, since the work force data used in Figure 3-3 are based primarily on wage and salary employment and do not include most of the self-employed commercial fishermen. Rogers estimated that there were nearly 3,000 commercial fishermen in Bristol Bay in the summer of 1970.[2] If commercial fishermen were added to the data in Figure 3-3, the

---

[1]Because of seasonal factors, the unemployment rates are probably overestimated and participation rates underestimated by the data in Table 3-1. The reason for this is that the 1970 census was taken on April 1, which is about the seasonal low point for employment in the Bristol Bay region. Generally, however, the comparison of the different rates at that point in time would still produce relevant results, particularly with regard to permanent or year-round employment opportunities.

[2]Rogers, *Labor Changes in Salmon Industry.*

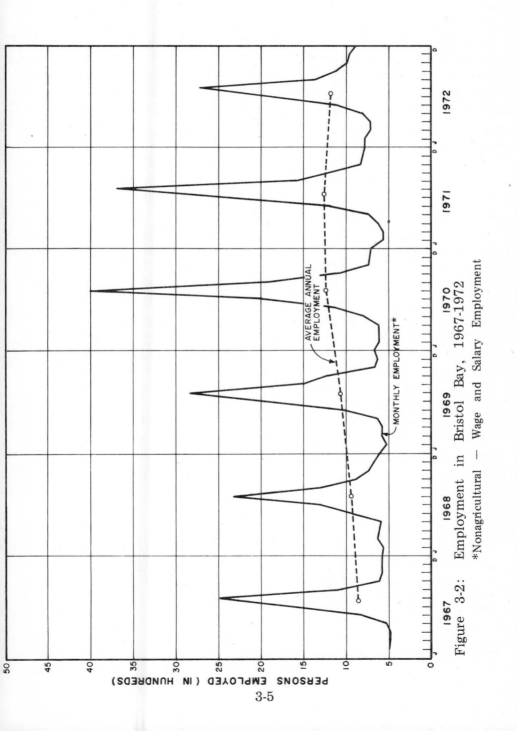

Figure 3-2: Employment in Bristol Bay, 1967-1972
*Nonagricultural — Wage and Salary Employment

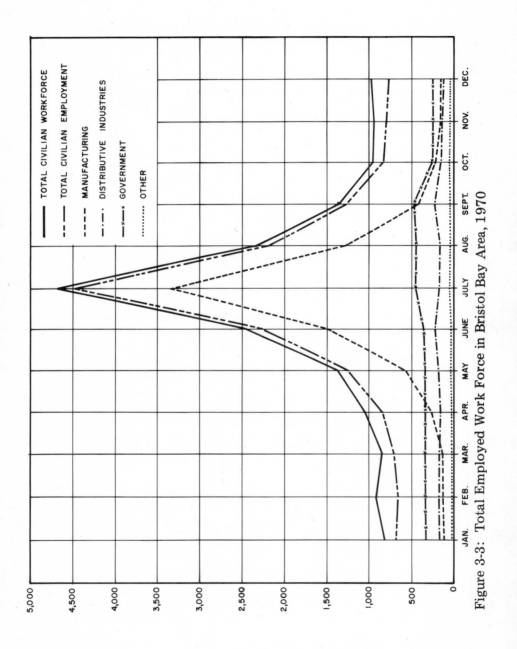

Figure 3-3: Total Employed Work Force in Bristol Bay Area, 1970

estimated labor force and employment would exceed 7,500 persons in July 1970.

Because the Bristol Bay economy depends upon the highly seasonal salmon fishery, a large proportion of the resident labor force is employed for only part of the year. During 1969, about 30 percent of the Bristol Bay population over sixteen years old were employed for thirteen weeks or less, and 36 percent were employed for forty weeks or more (see Table 3-2). In contrast, for the state as a whole, only 10 percent were employed for less than thirteen weeks, and 52 percent were employed for more than forty weeks. Among the Native population, the limited employment time is particularly striking. Of those who worked at all, fully 60 percent worked less than thirteen weeks. Clearly, on an annual basis, only a fraction of the available labor force was employed in the Bristol Bay region.

The local economy is affected not only by the seasonal fluctuations during the year but also by the inherent cyclic variability in the salmon run from year to year:

> The fish are well known to run in severe fluctuations of four or five year "cycles" which affects the personal income of most ... residents, and in poor years local purchasing power decreases. When this occurs people will cut down either on their consumption of goods, or take advantage of credit, or both. A small business affected so heavily by the variability of the salmon runs will find it difficult to operate under these circumstances, especially with the good years difficult to predict and the poor ones occurring frequently. As a result, the Borough can maintain only those retail stores and services that are reasonably certain of profitable survival, even during the period of two or three "bad catch" years.[3]

In view of the low income levels in Bristol Bay, the resident commercial fisherman must forego some necessary expenditures for food, clothing, and housing in order to buy a fishing boat and gear. If he cannot pay cash for the boat, he must make large annual payments until a loan is repaid. The fisherman often obligates nearly all of his capital to purchase highly specialized equipment which can

---

[3] ASHA *Bristol Bay Borough Dev. Plan*, p. 37.

Table 3-2
WORKERS BY WEEKS WORKED
BRISTOL BAY VERSUS ALASKA 1969

	Bristol Bay						Alaska					
	Total		White		Nonwhite		Total		White		Nonwhite	
	Number	Percent	Number	Percent	Number	Percent	Number	Percent	Number	Percent	Number	Percent
Male, 16 yrs. old and over	1,594		797		797		107,277		88,945		18,332	
40-52 weeks	742	46.5	600	75.3	142	17.8	75,249	70.1	67,992	76.4	7,257	39.6
14-39 weeks	273	17.1	105	13.2	168	21.1	15,219	14.2	11,591	13.0	3,628	19.8
13 weeks or less	451	28.3	80	10.0	371	46.5	9,253	8.6	4,374	4.9	4,879	26.6
Did Not Work	128	8.0	12	1.5	116	14.6	7,556	7.0	4,988	5.6	2,568	14.0
Female, 16 yrs. old and over	1,046		296		750		83,850		67,631		16,219	
40-52 weeks	198	18.9	113	38.2	85	11.3	24,023	28.6	21,337	31.5	2,686	16.6
14-39 weeks	111	10.6	61	20.6	50	6.7	14,637	17.5	12,165	18.0	2,472	15.2
13 weeks or less	348	33.3	34	11.5	314	41.9	10,647	12.7	7,602	11.2	3,045	18.8
Did Not Work	389	37.2	88	29.7	301	40.1	34,543	41.2	26,527	39.2	8,016	49.4
Total, 16 yrs. old and over	2,640		1,093		1,547		191,127		156,576		34,551	
40-52 weeks	940	35.6	713	65.2	227	14.7	99,272	51.9	89,329	57.1	9,943	28.8
14-39 weeks	384	14.5	166	15.2	218	14.1	29,856	15.6	23,756	15.2	6,100	17.7
13 weeks or less	799	30.3	114	10.4	685	44.3	19,900	10.4	11,976	7.6	7,924	22.9
Did Not Work	517	19.7	100	9.1	417	27.0	42,099	22.0	31,515	20.1	10,584	30.6

Sources: U.S. Department of Commerce, Bureau of the Census, 1970 Census, Alaska, Table 56; 1970 Census, Alaska, special computer runs; 1970 Census United States Summary, Table 93.

only be used during the brief salmon season. Even in a bonanza year, the fisherman may have to allocate a major portion of his earnings to cover the indebtedness of former seasons. In a bad year, he may fall behind in his payments, and a string of bad years may cause him financial disaster.

Employment by Industry

Employment in each of the major industries in the Bristol Bay area is shown in Table 3-3 for the period from 1961 to 1972. The discussion below outlines the factors which have produced the observed development of each sector.

Manufacturing

In Bristol Bay, manufacturing is synonymous with salmon processing. Between 1961 and 1972, the industry averaged 53 percent of the total wage and salary employment; however, this proportion does seem to be declining somewhat over time. In 1961, 58 percent of total employment was in manufacturing, compared to 34 percent in 1972. Even in 1970, when Bristol Bay experienced the largest salmon harvest in history, manufacturing employment averaged only 55 percent of the total.

Due to the highly seasonal nature of the industry, computing average annual employment by adding average monthly employment and dividing by twelve grossly underestimates the importance of seafood processing. For example, in 1972, an "average" of 402 people were employed in manufacturing, but the average monthly employment ranged from thirty-eight persons in March to 1,835 persons in July. The employment during the peak month gives a closer approximation to the number of people engaged in seafood processing in the course of a year.

Alaska's employment statistics also understate the impact of the fishing industry, because there has been no reliable estimate of direct employment in commercial fishing. Since most commercial fishermen are self-employed, they are generally not included in the estimates of total employment. In 1970, Rogers estimated that 2,980

Table 3-3

NONAGRICULTURAL WAGE AND SALARY EMPLOYMENT BY INDUSTRY

BRISTOL BAY LABOR AREA

	1961	1962	1963	1964	1965	1966	1967	1968	1969	1970	1971	1972
					Number Employed							
TOTAL EMPLOYMENT	897	765	780	743	1084	1022	866	943	1062	1253	1242	1171
Manufacturing	525	370	382	334	626	515	371	418[b]	515[b]	691[b]	638[b]	402
Transportation, Communication, and Public Utilities	65	67	68	73	89	94	95	113	117	110	110	104
Trade	39	34	28	24	29	28	30	35	42	47	46	59
Service	28[c]	24[c]	22[c]	31[c]	31	27	38	29	25	23	33	45
Government	229	251	270	275	287	309	317	340	336	366	384	488
Other[a]	11	19	10	6	22	49	15	8[b]	27[b]	16[b]	31[b]	73
					Percentage Employed							
Manufacturing	58.5	48.4	49.0	45.0	57.7	50.4	42.8	44.3	48.5	55.1	51.4	34.3
Transportation, Communication, and Public Utilities	7.2	8.6	8.7	9.8	8.2	9.2	10.1	12.0	11.0	8.8	8.9	8.9
Trade	4.3	4.4	3.6	3.2	2.7	2.7	3.5	3.7	4.0	3.8	3.7	5.0
Service	3.1	3.1	2.8	4.2	2.9	2.6	4.4	3.1	2.4	1.8	2.7	3.8
Government	25.5	32.8	34.6	37.0	26.5	30.2	36.6	36.1	31.6	29.2	30.9	41.7
Other	1.2	2.5	1.3	0.8	2.0	4.8	1.7	0.8	2.5	1.3	2.5	6.2

Source : Alaska Department of Labor, "Workforce Estimates."

fishermen were employed in Bristol Bay during July.[4] This implies that the work force estimates shown in Table 3-3 underestimate the importance of the fishing industry by nearly 50 percent.

Trade and Service

Trade and service firms account for relatively small proportions of Bristol Bay's employment. The number of persons employed in trade rose from thirty-nine in 1961 to fifty-nine in 1972, while service employment increased from twenty-eight to forty-five persons. The month-to-month variation in these industries is minimal and does not follow a consistent pattern from year to year. There are eighteen retail trade firms in Bristol Bay, a third of which are eating and drinking establishments. Most of the stores are located in Dillingham or the Bristol Bay Borough, but Togiak and Manokotak have village cooperative stores.

Transportation, Communication, and Public Utilities

The number of persons employed in transportation, communication, and public utilities rose from sixty-five in 1961 to 104 in 1972. In that interval, the proportion of employment in these industries rose from 7.2 percent to 8.9 percent of the total work force. There is some decline in employment during the winter months, but the seasonal variation is not very large. Transportation companies in Bristol Bay include three airlines, two air-taxi services, a taxicab company, and two lighterage firms. There are two electric companies and one telephone utility, but no commercial radio or television stations.

Government Employment

Government has traditionally been one of the most important employers in Alaska's economy. In Bristol Bay, the fishing industry accounts for the largest proportion of total annual employment, but government offers the greatest number of year-round jobs. In many

---

[4] Rogers, *Labor Changes in Salmon Industry.*

of the small villages, the only persons with wage income throughout the year are the postmaster, health aide, school teachers and other school employees. From 1961 to 1972, the government has accounted for roughly one-third of the total employment in the Bristol Bay region (see Table 3-3).

In 1972, the federal government employed 170 persons (see Table 3-4). The Kanakanak Public Health Service Hospital, Federal Aviation Agency, and civilian Air Force personnel accounted for most of these positions. Other federal employment in Bristol Bay was provided by the U.S. Post Office, U.S. Weather Bureau, U.S. Fish and Wildlife Service, and the National Park Service. Of the 197 state personnel in 1972, about 57 percent were teachers, administrators, and other employees of the state-operated school system which maintains nineteen village schools in Bristol Bay. The State Departments of Public Works, Health and Social Services, Fish and Game, and Highways averaged at least ten employees each. Local government employment in 1972 averaged 121 persons. Virtually all of this employment was concentrated in the city of Dillingham or the Bristol Bay Borough, which has its headquarters in Naknek. The 1970 census reported that government employment in Bristol Bay accounted for 50 percent of the male work force and 57 percent of the female (see Table 3-5). However, these proportions are inflated because the percentages were based solely on employment during the reference week (around April 1, 1970), when employment in the commercial fishing and fish processing industry was very low. The census information does, however, provide a good measure of the composition of permanent, year-round employment. It is apparent that the proportion of year-round employment attributable to the government sector is much higher in Bristol Bay than in the rest of Alaska or the U.S. It is also interesting to note that white employees hold over half of the government jobs, although whites account for only 28 percent of the civilian population. There is a particularly high proportion of whites employed by local government units; only 28 percent of the jobs in local government are held by Natives.

Table 3-4

GOVERNMENT EMPLOYMENT 1972 BRISTOL BAY LABOR MARKET AREA

	Jan.	Feb.	Mar.	Apr.	May	June	July	Aug.	Sept.	Oct.	Nov.	Dec.	Annual Average
State Government	177	199	190	199	187	185	136	153	207	221	250	254	197
Governor's Office	3	16	3	3	2	1	1	1	1	1	1	1	3
Health and Social Services	11	11	13	14	12	12	12	15	13	12	11	12	12
Labor	1	1	1	1	1	1	1	1	1	1	1	1	1
Public Safety	6	6	7	7	5	6	5	11	9	8	10	10	8
Public Works	26	33	25	25	25	21	20	21	28	27	26	27	25
Highways	7	7	7	7	8	8	13	25	28	24	24	11	14
State Operated Schools	101	108	118	129	119	121	70	65	112	123	148	141	113
Community and Regional Affairs	–	–	–	–	–	–	–	–	–	10	15	36	20
Legislative Affairs	2	2	2	2	2	2	2	2	2	2	2	2	2
Court System	3	3	3	3	3	3	3	3	3	3	3	3	3
Federal Government (civilian)	153	155	160	149	157	169	165	169	167	203	197	199	170
Transportation	53	51	51	50	49	50	49	49	48	47	49	48	50
Air Force	53	58	60	53	57	57	54	53	52	46	40	46	52
Interior	12	13	14	14	15	25	23	25	22	11	12	11	16
Commerce	8	8	8	6	8	9	11	16	17	7	10	10	10
Post Office	27	25	27	26	28	28	28	26	28	28	26	28	27
Health Education and Welfare	–	–	–	–	–	–	–	–	–	64	60	56	60
Local Government	119	110	121	132	116	92	107	112	137	141	134	136	121
Military													435

Source: Alaska Department of Labor.

Table 3-5
CLASS OF WORKER
BRISTOL BAY – 1970

Class of Worker	Bristol Bay						Alaska			U.S.
	Total		White		Nonwhite		Total	White	Nonwhite	Total
	Number	Percent	Number	Percent	Number	Percent	Percent	Percent	Percent	Percent
Males										
Employed, 16 years old and over	439		238		201					
Employee of Private Company	167	38.0	77	32.4	90	44.7	57.8	59.0	48.0	75.5
Government Employees	223	50.8	132	55.5	91	45.3	33.6	31.9	47.0	14.1
Federal	100	22.7	66	27.7	34	16.9	17.1	15.8	27.1	4.6
State	81	18.5	34	14.3	47	23.4	9.4	9.0	12.2	3.4
Local	42	9.6	32	13.4	10	5.0	7.2	7.1	7.7	6.1
Self Employed Workers	49	11.2	29	12.2	20	10.0	8.4	8.9	4.9	10.2
Unpaid Family Workers	—	—	—	—	—	—	0.2	0.2	0.2	0.2
Females										
Employed, 16 years old and over	305		159		146					
Employee of Private Company	113	37.0	60	37.7	53	36.3	53.9	55.0	46.9	75.9
Government Employees	174	57.0	81	50.9	93	64.0	40.9	39.6	49.0	19.5
Federal	67	22.0	16	10.1	51	34.9	17.0	15.5	26.2	3.8
State	37	12.1	16	10.1	21	14.4	11.5	10.9	15.1	4.9
Local	70	23.0	49	30.8	21	14.4	12.5	13.2	7.7	10.8
Self Employed Workers	18	5.9	18	11.3	—	—	4.3	4.5	3.1	3.7
Unpaid Family Workers	—	—	—	—	—	—	0.9	0.9	1.0	1.0
Total										
Employed, 16 years old and over	744		397		347					
Employee of Private Company	280	37.6	137	34.5	143	41.2	56.2	57.5	47.5	75.7
Government Employees	397	53.3	213	53.6	184	53.0	36.5	34.9	47.9	16.1
Federal	167	22.4	82	20.7	85	24.5	17.1	15.7	26.7	4.3
State	118	15.9	50	12.6	68	19.6	10.2	9.7	13.5	3.9
Local	112	15.0	81	20.4	31	8.9	9.3	9.5	7.7	7.9
Self Employed Worker	67	9.0	47	11.8	20	5.8	6.8	7.2	4.1	7.7
Unpaid Family Workers	—	—	—	—	—	—	0.5	0.4	0.6	0.5

Sources: U.S. Department of Commerce, Bureau of the Census, 1970 Census, Alaska, Table 56; 1970 Census, Alaska, special computer runs; 1970 Census, United States Summary, Table 93.

Distribution of Income

The 1970 census estimated that median family income in Bristol Bay for 1969 was $7,785 (see Table 4-1), about 60 percent below the median family income for the state as a whole. As shown in Table 4-1, the distribution of income in Bristol Bay differs from the statewide pattern. Roughly one-third of the families in Bristol Bay have incomes less than $5,000; one-third, $10,000 and above; and one-third in the intermediate range. By comparison, the statewide data show that 14 percent of the families fall in the low income bracket, 24 percent in the intermediate bracket and 62 percent in the higher bracket. The income patterns of Bristol Bay white families more closely approximate the state distribution, except that there is a larger proportion in the lower income categories than for whites statewide. Income levels of Bristol Bay Native families are very low. Only 15 percent of Native families have incomes in excess of $10,000—a figure less than half the statewide average for nonwhites. Nearly 30 percent of Bristol Bay's Native families have annual incomes below $3,000. The median income for Natives in Bristol Bay is under $6,000, which is less than half of the statewide median for all families and almost $2,000 less than the state median for nonwhite families.

Earnings and Wage Rates

The earnings data in Table 4-2 show that the observed differences in regional income are not due solely to differences in the relative importance of various occupations. There is a consistent

Table 4-1
INCOME OF FAMILIES
BRISTOL BAY 1970

	Bristol Bay						Alaska		
	Total Families		White		Nonwhite		Total	White	Nonwhite
	Number	Percent	Number	Percent	Number	Percent	Percent	Percent	Percent
Less than $1,000	62	8.1	18	5.7	44	9.8	2.2	1.6	5.6
$1,000 to 1,999	45	5.9	5	1.6	40	8.9	2.3	1.4	7.5
2,000 to 2,999	53	6.9	5	1.6	48	0.7	2.7	1.7	8.3
3,000 to 3,999	42	5.5	11	3.5	31	6.9	3.2	2.2	8.6
4,000 to 4,999	42	5.5	10	3.2	32	7.1	3.7	7.0	3.7
5,000 to 5,999	52	6.8	6	1.9	46	10.2	5.0	4.3	8.8
6,000 to 6,999	76	9.9	15	4.8	61	13.6	4.9	4.6	6.8
7,000 to 7,999	37	4.8	15	4.8	22	4.9	4.6	4.5	5.2
8,000 to 8,999	50	6.5	5	1.6	45	10.0	4.8	4.7	4.9
9,000 to 9,999	28	3.7	12	3.8	16	3.6	4.3	4.3	4.4
10,000 to 14,999	167	21.8	134	42.5	33	7.3	24.6	25.5	19.2
15,000 to 24,999	101	13.2	74	23.5	27	6.0	28.2	31.3	11.0
25,000 or more	10	1.3	5	1.6	5	1.1	9.6	10.9	1.9
TOTAL	765	x100.0	315	100.0	450	100.0	100.0	100.0	100.0
Median Income	$7,785						$12,443	$13,464	

Grouped bracket percentages:

Total Families: 20.9; 31.7; 36.3
White (Bristol Bay): 8.9 / 15.6; 31.9; 16.9; 67.6
Nonwhite (Bristol Bay): 29.4; 43.4; 42.3; 14.4
Alaska Total: 7.2; 14.1; 23.6; 62.4
Alaska White: 4.7; 9.9; 22.4; 67.7
Alaska Nonwhite: 21.4 / 9.9; 30.1; 32.1; 37.7

Sources: U.S. Department of Commerce, Bureau of the Census, *1970 Census*, Alaska, special computer runs, *1970 Census*, Alaska, Table 47.

Table 4-2

EARNINGS BY OCCUPATION GROUPS

BRISTOL BAY 1970

Median earnings for selected occupation groups	Bristol Bay Borough	Bristol Bay Division	Bristol Bay Total	Alaska
Male, 16 years old and over with earnings	$ 8,800	$ 6,212	$ 6,859	$11,242
Professional and managerial	10,147	10,794	10,581	13,796
Craftsmen and foremen	11,176	7,600	8,479	12,098
Operatives	—	—	—	9,566
Laborers	2,250	4,400	4,179	6,747
Female, 16 years old and over over with earnings	2,200	4,500	4,092	4,818
Clerical and kindred workers	—	1,885	1,885	5,296
Operatives	—	—	—	2,274

Source: U.S. Department of Commerce, Bureau of the Census, *1970 Census*, Alaska, Tables 57 and 122.

earnings differential in virtually all occupational categories. Although there is considerable variation in the size of this gap, males in Bristol Bay typically earn about 40 percent less than the statewide average; females earn 25 percent below the state level.

Table 4-3 gives Bristol Bay average annual wage rates by industry for the 1960-72 period. The following discussion of wage rates lists the industries in descending order from the highest total payroll in 1972 to the lowest. In 1972, manufacturing (fish processing) ranked first with a payroll of $4.2 million, but 70 percent of these wages were earned in July, August, and September (see Table 4-4 for payrolls by quarter 1968-72). Manufacturing has been the most unstable of Bristol Bay industries, a reflection of the cyclic nature of seafood processing. Annual earnings in manufacturing peaked in 1960, 1965, and 1970—years of peak salmon runs in the Bristol Bay region. The average earnings in manufacturing shown in Table 4-3 were computed by dividing the total payroll for the year by the employment during the peak month of the salmon run. As was discussed in Chapter 3, the seasonal nature of the salmon fishery makes it inappropriate to measure employment by computing an annual average of monthly employment levels. Employment during the peak month is a more accurate measure of the number of people who earn income through employment in seafood processing.

The payroll for state and local government in 1972 was $3.3 million. Since 1967, the annual average wage for state and local government workers has steadily increased from $6,000 to $10,500 in 1970, a rise of 75 percent. Over this same period, the total payroll nearly tripled. Prior to 1969, the total payroll of federal government workers exceeded that of state and local government employees. In addition, the average annual wage in federal employment exceeded that of state and local government workers through 1971. Between 1971 and 1972, the average annual federal wage dropped from $11,900 to $9,900. In that same interval, the average state and local government wage rose from $10,000 to $10,500. The federal, state,

Table 4-3
BRISTOL BAY AREA AVERAGE ANNUAL WAGE
1960-1972

	1960	1961	1962	1963	1964	1965	1966	1967	1968	1969	1970	1971	1972
Industrial Classification													
Manufacturing[a]	$3295	2278	1631	1501	1565	2348	1606	1496	1589	1695	2254	1944	1529
Transportation, Communication, & Public Utilities	6453	6582	7127	5384	5820	5631	5889	6517	5903	6723	7339	8085	8858
Wholesale & Retail Trade	4012	4851	3797	4124	3746	3921	4661	4243	4062	4154	4280	5148	4382
Services	3130[b]	5090[b]	2504	2558	3726	3820	3668	3580	4321	4432	5438	4327	4452
Federal Government	—	—	—	—	6260	5334	5852	6997	7281	7622	9459	11917	9921
State & Local Government	—	—	—	—	3500	5397	5262	6000	6702	7261	8352	10027	10505

Source: Alaska, Department of Labor, Statistical Quarterly, 1960-72.

Table 4-4

QUARTERLY PAYROLLS BY INDUSTRY
BRISTOL BAY 1968-1972

	Total	Manufacturing	Transportation, Communication, & Public	Wholesale & Retail Trade	Services	Federal Government	State & Local Government
1968							
First Quarter	$ 910,950	—	$134,244	$ 31,603	$ 35,233	$ 288,784	$ 262,956
Second Quarter	1,527,224	685,875	159,862	33,038	27,795	341,523	272,016
Third Quarter	3,432,951	2,548,150	211,219	39,465	32,687	275,602	312,042
Fourth Quarter	1,160,237	—	161,777	37,817	29,590	311,077	319,171
Total	7,031,362	—	677,066	142,193	125,305	1,215,986	1,166,185
1969							
First Quarter	926,243	—	153,182	34,493	21,305	320,170	294,158
Second Quarter	1,694,257	788,637	202,124	43,608	25,520	301,762	313,799
Third Quarter	4,494,796	3,465,212	237,503	48,149	30,467	294,887	374,075
Fourth Quarter	1,284,025	—	193,835	48,224	33,515	285,972	397,530
Total	8,399,321	—	786,644	174,474	110,807	1,112,791	1,379,562
1970							
First Quarter	1,138,164	209,423	156,534	36,225	24,333	328,037	375,876
Second Quarter	2,612,783	1,451,169	215,500	45,745	24,840	464,942	397,315
Third Quarter	8,129,496	6,808,413	257,985	63,430	38,905	478,375	427,076
Fourth Quarter	1,670,392	—	177,277	55,783	47,009	261,056	503,636
Total	13,550,835	—	807,296	201,183	125,087	1,532,410	1,703,903
1971							
First Quarter	1,229,243	35,757	176,552	48,314	19,891	270,580	620,218
Second Quarter	2,891,692	1,348,698	230,168	56,320	41,923	548,625	596,017
Third Quarter	6,869,187	5,530,108	265,437	65,983	52,166	333,118	503,792
Fourth Quarter	1,705,742	—	217,205	66,180	61,825	277,707	827,123
Total	12,695,864	—	889,362	236,797	175,805	1,430,030	2,647,150
1972							
First Quarter	1,593,013	95,300	190,727	63,238	30,220	386,757	816,112
Second Quarter	2,531,425	926,677	214,172	93,781	41,970	372,129	770,362
Third Quarter	4,975,612	2,895,064	273,902	78,725	59,794	419,029	764,422
Fourth Quarter	2,260,529	242,135	242,458	90,215	68,348	518,736	979,412
Total	11,360,579	4,159,176	921,259	325,959	200,332	1,696,651	3,330,308

and local government wages are the most important source of stable year-round income in Bristol Bay.

Transportation, communications, and public utility wages, after moving erratically in earlier years, have increased steadily between 1969 and 1972. Average wages in the industry rose 32 percent during this period to an average annual wage of $8,858. The total payroll in 1972 was $921,000. Wholesale and retail trade wages have remained virtually constant. In 1960, the average worker in these industries earned $4,012; in 1972, the average annual earnings were $4,382, with an average of $4,260 over the twelve-year period. Total payroll in 1972 was $326,000. Services ranked last with a 1972 payroll of $200,000. Average annual wages in service industries increased steadily from $3,580 in 1967 to $5,327 in 1971, but fell to $4,452 in 1972, just slightly above earnings in the trade sector.

Public Assistance Income

The 1970 census reported that one sixth of the Bristol Bay families received public assistance or public welfare income in the preceding year (see Table 4-5). This is more than three times the statewide average. Of those families receiving assistance, 96 percent were Natives. About 27 percent of all Native families in Bristol Bay received some public assistance income. For the state as a whole, 21 percent of the nonwhite families receive some form of public assistance or welfare payments.

Bureau of Indian Affairs general assistance, state public assistance, and the federally funded food stamp program provide the three major forms of public assistance available to Bristol Bay residents. The state public assistance programs include payments for old age assistance, aid to the blind, aid to the disabled, and aid to dependent children. Table 4-6 shows the number of cases and dollar payments in each category for October 1970, 1971, and 1972. For October 1972, the total amount of state public assistance in Bristol Bay was $35,529. Comparable statistics are not available for years prior to 1970 because regulations for receiving assistance under these

Table 4-5
SOURCES OF FAMILY INCOME
BRISTOL BAY   1970

| | Bristol Bay | | | | | | Alaska | | |
| | Total | | White | | Nonwhite | | Total | White | Nonwhite |
	Number	Percent	Number	Percent	Number	Percent	Percent	Percent	Percent
Total Families	765	100.0	315	100.0	450	100.0	100.0	100.0	100.0
Wage and Salary	663	86.7	282	89.5	381	84.7	94.8	95.3	91.8
Self Employment	337	44.1	134	42.5	203	45.1	14.9	15.3	12.7
Social Security or Railroad Retirement	99	12.9	26	8.3	73	16.2	5.5	4.4	11.6
Public Assistance or Welfare Payments	128	16.7	5	1.6	123	27.3	4.9	2.0	20.8
All Other Income	122	15.9	38	12.1	84	18.7	27.5	29.3	17.4

Source: Alaska, Department of Labor, *Statistical Quarterly*, 1968-72.

Table 4-6

PUBLIC ASSISTANCE

BRISTOL BAY, OCTOBER 1970, 1971, 1972

	Number of Cases				Dollar Payments				
	OAA[a]	AB[b]	AD[c]	AFDC[d]	TOTAL	OAA	AB	AD	AFDC	TOTAL
1970	37	6	12	61	116	$5,383	$1,175	$2,320	$15,532	$24,410
1971	59	4	26	75	164	8,188	805	4,492	18,402	31,887
1972	73	4	30	95	202	8,670	805	4,870	21,184	35,529

[a]Old age assistance
[b]Aid to the blind
[c]Aid to the disabled
[d]Aid for dependent children

Source: Alaska, Department of Health and Social Services, Division of Family and Children Services, "October Report," 1970, 71, 72.

programs were changed in that year. Between 1970 and 1972, the number of Bristol Bay residents receiving state assistance increased from 116 to 202, and the amount of dollar payments rose from $24,410 to $35,529. The Department of Health and Social Services does not provide data on yearly total assistance, but if the October 1972 figure is typical, we can infer that the programs distributed about $426,000 to Bristol Bay in 1972.

Bureau of Indian Affairs general assistance is available only to Natives. In 1968, these outlays in Bristol Bay totaled $395,318 with payments to 367 cases (see Table 4-7). After that time, the number of cases and payments were cut sharply, and by 1971 total expenditure in Bristol Bay was only $46,065 and the case load was sixty-seven. In 1972, BIA assistance increased to 105 cases and total payments of $91,125.

The Food Stamp Bonus Coupon program receives funding from the U.S. Department of Agriculture but is administered by the state. Administration of this program for Bristol Bay recipients is handled through the Dillingham office of the Division of Family and Children's Services. During fiscal year 1969, the first full year the program was available to Bristol Bay residents, the bonus value of distributed coupons was $23,947. In fiscal year 1973, the bonus value of the coupons increased to $363,562 (see Table 4-8). Between July of 1972 and June of 1973, an average of 1,192 persons (241 households) in Bristol Bay received food stamps each month. This means that over one-fourth of the families in Bristol Bay received food stamps in that year. The bonus value of the coupons averaged $125 per family per month.

Generally, the salmon run peaks in July and results in high employment and incomes among the Bristol Bay residents. For example, in July 1972, only 266 Bristol Bay residents were using food stamps. In July 1973, however, due to a poor salmon run, the number of food stamp users jumped to 988.

It is anticipated that the percentage of Bristol Bay residents using food stamps will continue to rise. One state official said that

Table 4-7
BUREAU OF INDIAN AFFAIRS GENERAL ASSISTANCE
BRISTOL BAY COMMUNITIES, FISCAL YEARS 1968-1972

Community	FY 1968		FY 1969		FY 1970		FY 1971		FY 1972	
	Amount	Cases	Amount	Cases	Amount	Cases	Amount	Cases	Amount	Cases
Aleknagik	$ 27,137	26	—	—	6,113	9	—	—	—	—
Clarks Point	11,082	13	6,135	8	2,306	3	916	2	1,183	3
Dillingham	67,820	62	31,225	32	18,523	22	2,309	5	4,508	10
Egegik	18,039	19	3,301	5	1,279	2	1,861	2	6,620	6
Ekuk	2,840	4	639	2	—	—	—	—	—	—
Ekwok	22,453	20	20,447	15	29,458	14	5,363	6	3,005	3
Igiugig	6,879	5	7,962	6	5,542	5	1,476	1	3,900	2
Iliamna	9,783	9	8,495	5	400	1	1,128	3	5,041	4
King Salmon	—	—	121	1	1,002	1	—	—	—	—
Kanakanak	960	1	—	—	39	1	—	—	—	—
Kokhanok	12,458	9	11,410	8	9,912	7	984	1	10,646	7
Koliganek	11,527	11	12,733	11	11,005	9	2,306	4	3,116	3
Levelock	4,504	5	1,638	2	3,868	5	2,264	3	903	6
Manokotak	32,573	30	21,924	25	27,192	21	750	3	6,821	8
Naknek	—	—	—	—	—	—	—	—	1,225	1
South Naknek	12,645	8	3,400	4	4,376	4	260	2	284	1
North Naknek	—	—	2,090	2	—	—	262	1	—	—
Newhalen	4,050	3	3,214	3	1,288	1	1,000	1	4,976	3
New Stuyahok	41,892	28	29,041	29	64,067	28	1,916	4	1,491	1
Nondalton	36,112	33	46,193	28	6,512	12	17,845	13	28,188	26
Nushagak	—	—	310	1	—	—	—	—	—	—

(continued on next page)

Table 4-7 (continued from previous page)

Community	FY 1968		FY 1969		FY 1970		FY 1971		FY 1972	
	Amount	Cases	Amount	Cases	Amount	Cases	Amount	Cases	Amount	Cases
Pedro Bay	7,026	6	6,742	6	5,213	6	400	1	865	3
Pilot Point	2,980	9	693	2	1,458	4	1,637	5	1,993	1
Port Alsworth	–	–	–	–	–	–	488	1	840	1
Port Heiden	5,003	8	4,184	4	7,115	9	2,126	5	714	2
Togiak	54,666	51	22,078	25	15,496	15	302	2	4,506	13
Twin Hill	1,030	3	1,647	3	–	–	472	2	300	1
Ugashik	1,859	4	742	2	778	2	–	–	–	–
TOTAL	$395,318	367	$246,364	229	$222,933	181	$ 46,065	67	$ 91,125	105
Average Monthly Payment	90		90		102		57		72	

Source: U.S. Department of Interior, Bureau of Indian Affairs, Anchorage District Office (worksheets).

Table 4-8
PARTICIPATION IN THE FOOD STAMP PROGRAM
BRISTOL BAY, FISCAL YEAR 1972-73

Date	Number of Participants	Number of Households Participating	Dollar Value of Coupons	Cost to Recipients	Bonus Value of Coupons
July 72	226	64	10,392	2,078.75	8,313.25
Aug 72	916	169	29,279	4,143.75	25,135.25
Sept 72	938	188	30,598	4,180.50	26,417.50
Oct 72	1,284	253	41,588	6,262.75	35,325.25
Nov 72	1,364	272	44,980	7,643.00	37,337.00
Dec 72	1,321	271	43,183	7,696.00	35,487.00
Jan 73	1,335	273	43,125	9,778.75	33,346.25
Feb 73	1,387	285	44,544	11,509.75	33,034.25
Mar 73	1,397	286	45,232	12,704.25	32,211.75
Apr 73	1,411	286	45,514	13,274.00	32,240.00
May 73	1,400	278	44,703	12,500.00	32,213.00
June 73	1,328	261	42,509	9,997.25	32,511.75
Fiscal Year 1972 Totals	14,307	2,886	$ 465,647	$101,768.75	$363,562.25
Monthly Averages	1,192	241	38,804	8,480.73	30,296.85
July 73	988	183	33,457	5,207.00	28,248.00

Source: Rod Betit, Food Stamp Program Manager, Alaska Department of Health and Social Services, Division of Family and Children Services.

many residents are given the stamps outright because they have no money to buy them. The regulations governing the food stamp program have recently been revised to allow food stamps to be used for the purchase of nonfood items for subsistence hunting and fishing. However, stamps cannot be used for the purchase of guns or ammunition.[1]

Cost of Living

The *Quarterly Report on Alaska Food Prices* is the data series commonly used to make differential cost-of-living estimates between Alaska communities and other parts of the United States. The report is based on a national survey "market basket" of 45 food items. Unfortunately, no Bristol Bay community has regularly been surveyed in the report up to this time. However, a 1972 state employee cost-of-living study by the Alaska Division of Personnel did provide information on food costs in Dillingham (see Table 4-9). This survey found that food prices in Dillingham in October 1972 were 73 percent higher than in Seattle and 42 percent higher than in Anchorage.

Except for the food price information, the state cost-of-living survey covered state employees only. The survey measured food and beverage purchases (exclusive of alcoholic beverages, tobacco, and nonfood products) and made adjustments for special diets, hunting, fishing, gardening or maintenance of livestock. Housing expenditures included rent, mortgage payments, utilities, taxes, and insurance. The survey concluded that state employee food expenditures in Dillingham averaged $1,319 per person, about 35 percent higher than the Anchorage figure and statewide average (see Table 4-10). However, average annual housing expenditures of $1,041 per person in Dillingham were 6 percent less than the state average and 15 percent less than Anchorage. But this was because the houses in Dillingham tended to be smaller than average. Housing costs per square foot in

---

[1]Phyllis Williams, Alaska Department of Health and Social Services, Personal communication, 1974.

Table 4-9
RELATIVE COSTS OF FORTY-FOUR SELECTED FOOD ITEMS
IN FOURTEEN ALASKA CITIES AND TOWNS
OCTOBER 1972

City	Cost	Percent of Seattle	Percent of Anchorage
Soldotna	$38.36	137.1	112.1
Cordova	41.96	149.9	122.6
Palmer	35.49	126.8	103.7
Kenai	38.18	136.4	111.5
Fairbanks	37.91	135.5	110.8
Juneau	36.46	130.2	106.5
Anchorage	34.23	122.3	100.0
Ketchikan	35.38	126.5	103.4
Seward	37.80	135.0	110.4
Sitka	38.25	136.6	111.7
Haines	38.61	137.9	112.8
Bethel	53.61	191.5	156.6
Dillingham	48.44	173.1	141.5
Kodiak	39.12	139.8	114.3

Source: Alaska, Department of Administration, Division of Personnel, *Survey of Salaries and Benefits, Housing and Food Costs and Salary Recommendations*, Part III Housing and Food Costs, Juneau: December 1972.

Table 4-10
COSTS OF FOOD AND HOUSING FOR STATE EMPLOYEES 1972

	Dillingham		Dillingham/State Ratio		Dillingham/Anchorage Ratio		Statewide		Anchorage	
	Household	Person	Household	Person	Household	Person	Household	Person	Household	Person
Average Annual Food Expenditures	4,420	2,319	139	135	149	136	1,185	978	2,960	971
Average Annual Housing Expenditures	3,489	1,041	97	94	94	85	3,605	1,109	3,724	1,223
Average Housing cost per square foot	4.53	—	128	—	142	—	3.54	—	3.19	—

Source: Alaska, Department of Admininstration, Division of Personnel, *Survey of Salaries and Benefits, Housing and Food Costs and Salary Recommendations, Part III Housing and Food Costs*, Juneau, December 1972.

Dillingham were found to be 28 percent higher than statewide and 42 percent higher than Anchorage. Furthermore, the condition of housing in Dillingham was found to be lower than in Anchorage, so 42 percent is actually an underestimate of the true differential in cost of housing. Based on the study's findings, the Division of personnel recommended that wages of Bristol Bay state employees should be about 34 percent higher than those of state employees living in Anchorage.

Housing

Housing in Bristol Bay is commonly overcrowded, dilapidated, and in short supply. The *1970 Census of Housing* reported that 53 percent of the housing units lacked piped-in water, an amenity present in all but 12 percent of the households statewide and all but about 2 percent nationally (see Table 5-1). Only 42 percent of Bristol Bay's housing units had complete kitchen facilities, which is less than half the state and national averages. Most of the better housing in the region is concentrated in Dillingham, Naknek, and King Salmon. Families with better housing characteristically have higher incomes, greater educational attainment, and are white.[1]

A basic obstacle to improving housing conditions is the instability in the local economy due to the seasonal nature of the fishing industry. Sources of credit are inadequate, and very few homes are purchased through banks or other financing.[2] High construction and maintainance costs are also a problem. Much of the higher construction costs are attributable to transportation costs. The area lacks a highway or rail connection with major sources of supply. Most construction materials are brought in by boat during the brief ocean shipping season. The cargo must be lightered to shore or brought in by barge. Shipping to the more distant points in the region increases the transportation costs even more. An additional obstacle to better housing arises from the fact that the fishing season

---

[1]ASHA *Bristol Bay Borough Development Plan*, p. 138, and ASHA *Dillingham Plan*, p. 60.

[2]ASHA *Dillingham Plan*, p. 64.

Table 5-1
HOUSING CHARACTERISTICS
BRISTOL BAY CENSUS DIVISION   1970

	Borough		Division		Total		Alaska	U.S.
	Number	Percent	Number	Percent	Number	Percent	Percent	Percent
Total Population	11045		3587		4632			
All Year Round Housing Units	199	100.0	866	100.0	1065	100.0	100.0	100.0
Population								
Population in housing units in 1970	579		3550.0		4129.0		(276,918)	
Per occupied unit	3.4		4.0		4.5		3.5	
owner	3.8		5.1		—		3.8	
Piped Water in Structure								
Hot and Cold	134	67.3	268	30.9	402	37.7	85.8	95.2
Cold Only	16	8.0	83	9.6	99	9.3	2.6	2.3
None	49	24.6	515	59.5	564	53.0	11.6	2.4
Flush Toilet								
For exclusive use of household	136	68.3	282	32.7	418	20.2	85.3	95.0
Also used by another household	5	2.5	—	—	5	0.5	1.1	1.0
None	58	29.1	584	67.4	642	60.3	13.6	4.0
Bathtub or Shower								
For exclusive use of household	129	64.8	263	30.4	392	85.3	84.9	92.4
Also used by another household	5	2.5	—	—	5	0.5	1.1	1.0
None	65	32.7	603	69.6	668	62.7	14.0	4.8
Complete Kitchen Facilities								
For exclusive use of household	150	75.4	292	33.7	442	41.5	85.4	95.4
Also used by another household	—	—	—	—	—	—	0.3	0.2
No complete kitchen facilities	49	24.6	574	66.3	623	58.5	14.4	4.4

Table 5-1 (continued)

Rooms								
1 room	5	2.5	173	20.0	178	16.7	9.2	1.9
2 rooms	43	21.6	150	17.3	193	18.1	10.6	3.3
3 rooms	25	12.7	183	21.1	208	19.5	14.8	11.2
4 rooms	60	30.2	134	15.5	194	18.2	22.4	22.9
5 rooms	40	20.1	130	15.0	170	16.0	20.9	24.9
6 rooms	21	10.6	30	3.5	51	4.8	11.6	19.9
7 rooms	—	—	23	2.7	23	2.2	5.6	9.4
8 or more rooms	5	2.5	43	5.0	48	4.5	4.9	8.1
Persons								
All occupied units	169	100.0	747	100.0	916	100.0	100.0	100.0
1 person	17	10.1	113	15.1	130	14.2	13.7	17.6
2 persons	42	24.9	81	10.8	123	13.4	24.7	29.6
3 persons	45	26.6	70	9.4	115	12.6	17.3	17.2
4 persons	18	10.7	100	13.4	118	12.9	17.1	15.4
5 persons	21	12.4	111	14.9	132	14.4	12.1	9.8
6 persons	16	9.5	87	11.6	103	11.2	7.1	5.3
7 persons	10	5.9	82	11.0	92	10.0	4.5	2.7
8 or more persons	—	—	103	13.9	103	11.2	3.6	2.4
Persons per room								
All occupied units	169	100.0	747	100.0	916	100.0	100.0	100.0
1.00 or less	117	69.2	359	47.8	476	52.0	81.0	91.8
1.01 – 1.50	34	201.0	95	12.7	120	14.1	10.0	6.0
1.51 or more	18	10.7	293	39.2	311	34.0	9.0	2.2

Sources: U.S. Department of Commerce, Bureau of the Census, 1970 Census of Housing, Alaska, Table 32, 33, 37, 60, 63; 1970 Census of Housing, United States Summary, Tables 3, 4, and 24.

occurs during the months that are most favorable for housing construction.[3]

Even in Dillingham, the largest population center, housing conditions were described by the Alaska State Housing Authority (ASHA) as "a handicap to the welfare of the community."[4] An ASHA housing survey in 1970 revealed that 70 percent of all units were unsound. About 20 percent of Dillingham's housing was termed "dilapidated"—too costly to repair and often dangerous to health and safety. The remaining 50 percent was classified as "deteriorating,"—structurally sound but in need of repair.[5] The units were also more crowded than average with about four persons per unit, compared to an average 3.5 per unit statewide.[6] In addition to these poor conditions, housing is in short supply:

> There are virtually no houses of any kind of quality available for sale, and the vacancy rate is very low for rental units and apartments. There is a problem also which compounds the situation in the summer when the population nearly doubles during the fishing season.[7]

The ASHA study of Dillingham concluded that there was a need for low and middle income housing in Dillingham.[8] In 1971, the city approved a plan to establish Turnkey-type housing in Dillingham; however, the proposal fell through, and the housing conditions found in the 1970 ASHA survey have not changed much. However, in the

---

[3] Ibid.

[4] Ibid., p. 59.

[5] Ibid.

[6] Ibid., p. 61.

[7] Ibid.

[8] Ibid., p. 66.

past few years, some new homes have been constructed and several mobile homes have been brought in.[9]

In the Bristol Bay Borough, the best housing is found in King Salmon.[10] Most of this housing consists of apartment units with central water and sewer facilities. Housing units here are a combination of government built units, which are occupied by state and federal personnel, and privately owned, single-family dwellings. There are also some mobile homes in the community. An ASHA survey found that South Naknek had the poorest housing in the Borough. More than 84 percent of the units were inadequate in terms of size or facilities or both. Housing in Naknek falls in the intermediate range between South Naknek and King Salmon, with about 57 percent of the units classified by ASHA as inadequate.[11]

In the remote outlying villages, housing conditions vary widely, but on the whole are substandard. Since 1970, most of the new village housing units have been built at Manokotak, New Stuyahok, and Nondalton. In most of these communities, any major improvements in housing would also require electric power, piped-in water, and improved sewage disposal.[12]

Utilities

Dillingham is the only community in Bristol Bay which provides centralized water and sewer services. Even in Dillingham, however, many families are not served because they live in remote, low population areas of the city's twenty-two square mile boundaries. In 1970,

[9]Sam Coxson, Dillingham City Manager, personal communication, December 1973.

[10]ASHA *Bristol Bay Borough Development Plan*, p. 110.

[11]Ibid., pp. 120 and 137.

[12]Federal Field Committee for Development Planning in Alaska, *Community Inventory*, Anchorage, Alaska: 1971.

ASHA concluded that except for the city proper and Kanakanak:

> *The remainder of the township population is not, nor will it be in the near future, of sufficient density to justify additional or greatly extended community or centralized water or sewer systems.[13]*

Families in outlying areas of Dillingham use private wells and septic tanks or seepage pits. ASHA described Dillingham's water and sewer systems as being in a "sad state of repair." The city built an extended aeration sewage treatment facility, but it was oversized for the community's needs. The operating costs were so high that the plant was shut down in 1966 after only four months of operation. Since that time the plant has been bypassed and raw sewerage has been dumped into the Nushagak River. The water and sewer systems at Kanakanak are owned and operated by the U.S. Public Health Service. ASHA rated the systems as in "perfect condition" and termed the Dillingham water and sewer systems the "antithesis" of those at Kanakanak.[14]

The remainder of Bristol Bay's residents rely on private wells, rivers, streams, or springs for their water. In larger communities some residents have septic tanks, but sewage disposal is commonly primitive. One exception is the King Salmon Air Force Station which has its own water and sewer facility.[15]

The Nushagak Electric Cooperative, Inc., supplies power to Dillingham and Aleknagik; and the Naknek Electric Association supplies power to Naknek, South Naknek, and the village of King Salmon.[16] The Air Force Station at King Salmon has a self-contained power

---

[13]ASHA, *Dillingham Plan*, p. 93.

[14]Ibid.

[15]Public Information Officer, King Salmon Air Force Station, personal communication, August 1973.

[16]Dave Bouker, Nushagak Electric Cooperative, Inc., personal communication, October 1973.

plant.[17] The Alaska Village Electric Cooperative (AVEC) provides power for the communities of Togiak and New Stuyahok. AVEC has plans to extend service to Koliganek, Manokotak, and Nondalton in the near future.[18]

Dillingham, King Salmon, Naknek, and King Salmon Air Force Station have direct dial telephone service through North State Telephone Company.[19] All others rely on side-band radios or RCA bush radio telephone service. RCA's bush service is an automatic radio system which offers direct dialing capability. As of August 1973, RCA had installed bush phones in Egegik, South Naknek, Levelock, Igiugig, Kakhonak, Newhalen, Pedro Bay, and Nondalton. The company plans to extend service to Koliganek, Aleknagik, Twin Hills, Togiak and Manokotak in late 1973. The communities of Pilot Point, Port Alsworth, and Ugashik are scheduled to have bush radio phones installed in the spring of 1974.[20]

Medical Care

A devastating influenza epidemic which swept through Bristol Bay in 1918-19 wiped out several villages and decimated the population of others. In the aftermath, the Bureau of Education building at Kanakanak was enlarged and remodeled as a hospital to meet the chronic need for medical services in the area. The hospital was the first permanent health facility in Bristol Bay and has remained the major medical service center up to the present time. In 1932, the

---

[17]Public Information Officer, King Salmon Air Force Station, personal communication, August 1973.

[18]Dunkel Barger, Manager of Educational Programs for the Alaska Village Electric Coop, Inc., personal communication, August 1973.

[19]Caroline Gilbert, North State Telephone Company, personal communication, August 1973.

[20]Marie I. Morrison, Public Affairs, RCA Alaska communications, Inc., personal communication, August 1973.

small hospital was destroyed by fire but was replaced by a thirty-two bed unit in 1940.[21]

The Kanakanak hospital is now an Alaska Native Health Service Hospital administered by the Department of Indian Health of the United States Public Health Service. The hospital, which was renovated in 1972, has a bed capacity of twenty-nine and an average patient load of twelve. The hospital offers most general medical services including surgery, obstetrics, and treatment of communicable diseases. However, in cases requiring specialized surgery or extended medical care, patients are often sent to the U.S. Public Health Service Hospital in Anchorage. In addition to hospital services, the facility operates an outpatient public health service clinic. The clinic and hospital are staffed by two doctors and two dentists. Hospital and outpatient services are available to both Natives and non-Natives, though Natives have priority, and whites with the ability to pay are charged for services. A doctor in Dillingham operates a small clinic which offers the only private year-round medical services in Bristol Bay.[22]

Each of Bristol Bay's villages has a health aide who has been trained by the Indian Health Service under a program run by the Alaska Native Federation. Since few medical facilities have been built in the villages, the health aides operate out of their homes or the school. The health aides call the Kanakanak hospital on a regular basis via a radio communication system to report medical problems in the village and receive instructions. For cases requiring hospitalization or a doctor's care, patients are generally flown to Dillingham.[23]

In addition to village health aides, the services of itinerant nurses from the state Public Health Service are available on a regular

---

[21]Van Stone, *Eskimos*, p. 104.

[22]Lloyd Hermansen, Service Unit Director, Public Health Service, Alaska Native Hospital at Kanakanak, personal communication, August 1973.

[23]Ibid.

basis. The nurse stationed in Dillingham serves the city and the adjacent communities of Aleknagik, Clarks Point, Ekuk, and Portage Creek. Another Dillingham-based nurse serves Ekwok, Koliganek, Manokotak, New Stuyahok, Togiak, and Twin Hills. The communities of Naknek, Egegik, King Salmon, South Naknek, Levelock, Pilot Point and Port Heiden are served by a nurse stationed at the Public Health Center in Naknek, which has operated since 1948. During the fishing season, the services of a doctor employed by one of the canneries are also available. A public health nurse from Anchorage visits the Lake Iliamna communities of Igiugig, Iliamna, Newhalen, Kakhonak, Nondalton, and Pedro Bay.[24]

In 1973, the Bristol Bay Area Health Corporation (BBAHC) signed a contract with the Alaska Federation of Natives, Inc. (AFN) to coordinate a program for improved medical services in the region. AFN has provided $45,000 for the project and an additional $39,000 is being made available through government funding. The BBAHC plans to establish five-member health councils in each Bristol Bay village to define community health problems. Each council will have one member on the BBAHC Board. The corporation hopes that the Board will be able to influence the delivery of services and distribution of funds for the Kanakanak service unit. The BBAHC favors further training and higher pay for village health aides who currently earn $500 per month. The corporation noted that each village health aide sees about twenty patients per week and is also on call twenty-four hours a day and seven days a week.[25]

---

[24] Alaska Department of Health and Social Service.

[25] *Tundra Times*, October 3, 1973, p. 1.

CHAPTER 6
INDUSTRIAL ACTIVITY

Commercial Fishing and Fish Processing

Overview

The Bristol Bay economy is almost totally dependent upon fisheries, the salmon fishery, in particular. The region's fishery from 1961 through 1972 had an average wholesale value of $30 million.[1] In 1970, it had an average wholesale value of $48 million. However, the full economic impact of this value is not felt in Alaska because much of the money leaves the state as payments to nonresident workers, profits to outside companies, and purchases of supplies and equipment.[2]

Historically, the Bristol Bay fishery has followed a cyclic pattern. Rogers reports:

> The history of the Bristol Bay salmon fishery has been a pattern of boom, bust, and modest recovery typical of all Alaska fishing regions. From an annual average catch of four million fish for 1893-1900, the harvest rose to an average of twelve million for 1900-04, and with cyclical fluctuations, to an annual average of nineteen million fish for 1934-38. After that peak, there was a precipitous decline, but research and improved management programs in the 1950's led to a recovered annual average catch of nine million fish for the 1960's.[3]

---

[1] Alaska, Department of Fish and Game, "Area Management Report, Bristol Bay, 1972," unpublished.

[2] Rogers, *Labor Changes in Salmon Industry*, pp. 38-45.

[3] Ibid, p. 45.

Since 1970, the salmon catch has declined precipitously. In 1970, the catch amounted to approximately 22.1 million fish; it declined to 10.4 million fish in 1971, and in 1972 dropped to a record low of 2.4 million fish. The salmon catch in 1973 proved to be the worst on record for Bristol Bay, with only 1.5 million fish being harvested.[4]

The Bristol Bay region is divided into five fishing districts which encompass the area immediately adjacent to the mouths of the region's major river systems (see Map 6-1). The districts are the Naknek-Kvichak, Egegik, Ugashik, Nushagak, and Togiak. The Naknek-Kvichak district is the largest producer of red salmon, the most important species of the region. During the 1960's, this species accounted for 86 percent of the region's total salmon catch.[5]

The commercial fisheries harvest began in Bristol Bay in 1884 in the Nushagak district. At first, salmon were harvested with gill nets and traps. By the end of 1923, traps were prohibited and gill nets were then used exclusively. Power boats were introduced in 1922, but were immediately outlawed. This prohibition on power boats remained in effect until 1951. During this period most of the fishermen used sailboats. Staked or set gill nets were also used along the beaches during this time.[6]

Prior to World War II, except when there were complete closures, the number of fishing gear units in the region remained fairly constant. During the War, however, the number of units decreased significantly. Regulations were relaxed during the war years to permit use of motor-powered auxiliary vessels in the fishery to tow the sail-powered fishing vessels to and from the fishing grounds.

---

[4] Alaska, Department of Fish and Game, Division of Commercial Fisheries, Area Management Reports, 1970-74.

[5] Rogers, *Labor Changes in Salmon Industry*, p. 47.

[6] Alaska, Governor's Study Group on Limited Entry, *A Limited Entry Program for Alaska's Fisheries* (Juneau 1973) p. 234.

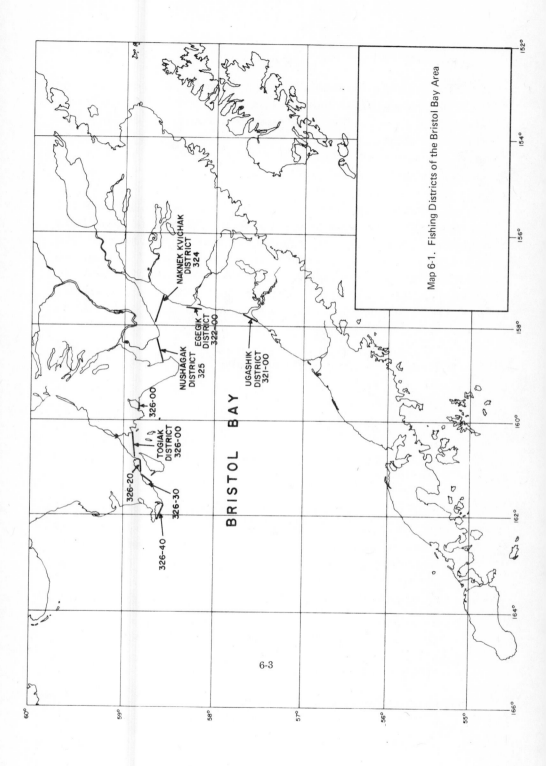

NAKNEK KVICHAK
DISTRICT
324

EGEGIK
DISTRICT
322-00

NUSHAGAK
DISTRICT
325

UGASHIK
DISTRICT
321-00

326-00

326-00

TOGIAK
DISTRICT
326-00

326-20

326-30

326-40

BRISTOL BAY

Map 6-1. Fishing Districts of the Bristol Bay Area

6-3

After the War, the number of fishing vessels at first increased slowly and then increased more rapidly with the legalizing of power fishing boats. During the 1960's the units of fishing gear used in Bristol Bay increased 100 percent.[7]

The regulation of fishing has undergone a significant change since statehood. Prior to statehood, fishing time was set before the run materialized and remained more or less constant. This had the effect of permitting gear to operate with equal pressure on all runs whether large or small. With the coming of statehood, however, the concept of the emergency order was introduced in which openings and closures were set from day to day, based upon daily information on catch figures and estimated escapements. These emergency orders have since been used to regulate fishing pressure on the red salmon runs, which usually last from three to four weeks.

Fishing activity in the region is intense, and the season is relatively short. An area biologist for the Alaska Department of Fish and Game reports:

> *Fishing activity commences in early June on king salmon with most effort concentrated in the Nushagak district. The king salmon run generally peaks during the last two weeks in June when effort then shifts to red salmon in all fishing districts. The red salmon run generally begins during the last week in June, peaks around July 4, and is essentially over by mid-July. Timing of the chum salmon and red salmon runs are nearly identical, although chum catches are usually sustained an additional week as red catches diminish. Pink salmon runs occur only during even years primarily in the Nushagak district. Pink fishing commences in mid-June and is essentially over by the second week in August. Minimal fishing activity exists on cohos after the pink salmon run diminishes. Residents of the Bristol Bay area comprise the bulk of the fishing effort on the coho salmon run, which begins in mid-July and lasts through the month of August. Peak catches are generally made from the last week of July through mid-August; however, timing varies considerably between districts.[8]*

---

[7] Ibid.

[8] ADF&G *Area Management Report, Bristol Bay,* 1972.

Value of Catch

The average yearly salmon catch from 1960 through 1971 amounted to 60 million pounds, having an average yearly value to fishermen of $12 million (see Table 6-1). The statistics for this period reflect the cyclic nature of the region's salmon fishery. The value to fishermen of other fish such as herring and bottom fish amounted to only $20 thousand in 1970 and $5 thousand in 1971, the only years for which figures are available.[9]

As shown in Table 6-2, canned salmon is the primary fish product of the Bristol Bay region. During the decade of the 1960's, over 95 percent of all the salmon caught was canned. In 1970 and 1971, about 90 percent of the catch was canned. Table 6-3 shows how the proportion of value added in canning salmon has changed over time relative to the value added by fishermen. In the years for which data are available, the share of value added attributable to both processing and prices paid to fishermen has remained rather constant. On the average, 54 percent of the wholesale cost of canned salmon results from processing and 46 percent is added by the price fishermen receive.

Other salmon products produced in Bristol Bay include fresh, frozen, and cured salmon and salmon roe. In 1971, the last year for which data are available, frozen salmon and salmon roe each amounted to 5 percent of the total processed salmon. Fresh salmon amounted to about 1 percent and cured salmon to 0.1 percent of the total production.

Other fish products produced in the region include cured herring and herring roe on kelp.[10] In 1970, the 7,000 pounds of cured herring prepared for market had a wholesale value to the processor of $0.22 per pound. Production of herring roe on kelp amounted to 40,000 pounds and had a wholesale value of $0.40 per pound.

---

[9] Rogers, *Labor Changes in Salmon Industry*, p. 48.

[10] Ibid., p. 49.

Table 6-1
BRISTOL BAY REGION
COMMERCIAL SALMON CATCH AND VALUE TO FISHERMEN
1960 — 1971

Year	Pounds	Value
1960	78,712,574	$ 14,253,471
1961	77,052,410	12,643,634
1962	35,463,811	5,770,382
1963	18,369,937	3,168,970
1964	41,533,243	7,351,301
1965	112,715,000	23,775,885
1966	68,884,072	11,807,385
1967	33,363,905	5,817,149
1968	26,485,303	5,595,575
1969	46,827,723	10,811,624
1970	116,440,704	27,028,586
1971	64,652,815	16,040,319
Average	60,041,791	12,013,690

Source: George W. Rogers, "A Study of the Socio-Economic Impact of Changes in the Harvesting Labor Force in the Alaska Salmon Industry," University of Alaska, Institute of Social, Economic and Government Research, December 1972.

Table 6-2
WHOLESALE VALUE OF SALMON PRODUCTS
BRISTOL BAY REGION — SELECTED YEARS

Product	Pounds	Total Value*	Wholesale Value per Pound	Percent of Total Salmon Catch
1962				
Fresh	—	—	—	—
Frozen	242,053	90,648	$ .37	1.10
Canned	22,956,048	15,441,397	.67	98.70
Cured	58,650	51,883	.88	.20
Roe	—	—	—	—
Total	23,256,751	15,583,878	.67	100.00
1964				
Fresh	6,000	2,400	.40	.02
Frozen	181,022	60,269	.33	.69
Canned	25,989,312	18,304,112	.70	98.52
Cured	166,178	105,078	.63	.60
Roe	37,453	14,860	.40	.14
Total	26,379,965	18,486,719	.70	100.00
1965				
Fresh	—	—	—	—
Frozen	377,024	138,850	.37	.52
Canned	72,207,312	53,428,291	.74	99.40
Cured	48,175	23,350	.48	.07
Roe	8,100	630	.08	.01
Total	72,640,611	53,591,121	.74	100.0
1966				
Fresh	26,822	10,878	.41	.06
Frozen	292,034	105,789	.36	.68
Canned	42,193,776	30,355,452	.72	98.81
Cured	16,333	10,561	.65	.04
Roe	173,660	164,435	.95	.41
Total	42,702,625	30,647,115	.72	100.00

(continued on next page)

Table 6-2 (continued from previous page)

Product	Pounds	Total Value*	Wholesale Value per Pound	Percent of Total Salmon Catch
1968				
Fresh	—	—	—	—
Frozen	858,750	300,870	.35	5.72
Canned	12,902,160	9,923,270	.77	86.05
Cured	575,418	215,672	.37	3.84
Roe	657,747	748,654	1.14	4.39
Total	14,994,075	11,188,486	.75	100.00
1970				
Fresh	170,000	151,229	.89	.26
Frozen	4,921,675	2,030,153	.41	7.53
Canned	58,219,392	45,915,431	.79	89.13
Cured	251,767	162,646	.65	.39
Roe	1,759,699	1,826,026	1.04	2.69
Total	65,322,726	50,085,485	.76	100.00
1971				
Fresh	324,039	127,978	.39	.79
Frozen	2,173,072	974,563	.45	5.20
Canned	37,181,088	33,227,107	.89	89.01
Cured	49,081	25,892	.53	.12
Roe	2,037,454	2,313,144	1.14	4.88
Total	41,764,734	36,668,684	.82	100.00

*Total value is wholesale value to processor

Source: Alaska, the Governor's Study Group on Limited Entry, *A Limited Entry Program for Alaska's Fisheries*, Juneau 1973.

Table 6-3
SHARES OF VALUE ADDED IN CANNED SALMON

Year	Total Pounds of Salmon Canned (Millions of pounds)	Wholesale Value Per Canned Pound	Value to Fishermen Per Processed Pound	Percent Value Added By Processing
1965	72.2	$ .74	$ .33	55
1966	42.2	.72	.28	61
1968	12.9	.75	.37	51
1970	58.2	.79	.41	48
1971	37.1	.89	.38	57

Source: George W. Rogers, "A Study of the Socio-Economic Impact of Changes in the Harvesting Labor Force in the Alaska Salmon Industry," (University of Alaska, Institute of Social,, Economic and Government Research, December 1972) Table 14, p. 48.

Fish Processing

The fish processing plants that operated in Bristol Bay in 1972 are listed in Table 6-4. Of the forty-five canning lines[11] available in the Bristol Bay region, only twenty-five were operated in 1972.[12] Most of the canneries processed salmon roe; three plants prepared fresh fish; four plants processed frozen and salted fish; and only one plant processed smoked salmon and herring products.

Processors recently constructed a $1.24 million cold storage plant with dock facilities at Dillingham. Due to engineering difficulties, however, this facility is now operating at only half capacity. At full capacity, it will be able to sharp freeze 40,000 pounds of fish every twenty-two hours. The plant processed only salmon during 1973. It shipped most of the processed king salmon to Denmark via Seattle. The frozen red, pink, and chum salmon it sold to the Japanese market. The plant plans to expand operations in 1974 to include freezing of tanner crabs.[13]

The state of Alaska has an administrative policy, with no statutory support, that requires that salmon and most other fishery resources be primary processed prior to their export from the state. A study made in 1970 has concluded that the primary processing policy in effect subsidizes the fish processors of the state at the expense of Alaska's fishermen. The study indicates that this policy prevents the purchase of fresh fish by Japanese freezer ships which pay higher prices for salmon than do domestic processors, and that prices paid for salmon remain at the level set by established operators. This difference in price represents a cost to the fishermen, most of whom are state residents. It also represents a cost to the state economy, because the policy subsidizes a processing industry which,

---

[11] One line performs the complete cleaning and processing operation.

[12] ADF&G *Area Management Report, Bristol Bay*, 1972.

[13] "Bristol Bay Fishermen Look Toward Better Future," *Anchorage Daily Times* (August 6, 1973) p. 9.

Table 6-4
FISH PROCESSING PLANTS
BRISTOL BAY 1972

Operation	Salmon Products						Herring Products	
	Canned	Fresh	Frozen	Smoked	Salted	Eggs	Cured	Eggs
Alaska Packers Assoc., Inc., So. Naknek	X					X		
Bumble Bee Seafoods, Naknek	X					X		
Cascade America, Nushagak River			X			X		
Clark Fishing and Packing, Egegik					X			
Columbia Wards Fisheries, Ekuk	X		X			X		
Grindle Saltry, Egegik					X			
Kachemak Seafoods, Togiak			X		X			
Kayak Packing Company, Naknek River	X					X		
Marubeni America Corp., Bristol Bay						X		
Mitsui and Company, Naknek						X		
Nelbro Packing Company, Naknek	X					X		
New England Fish Company, Egegik	X					X		
Peter Pan Seafoods, Inc., Naknek	X					X		
W. A. Peterson Company, Egegik				X				
Queen Fisheries, Inc., Nushagak	X					X		
Red Salmon Company, Naknek	X					X		
Surfline Seafood, Naknek					X	X		
Togiak Fisheries, Inc., Togiak	X	X	X					
Western Alaska Enterprises, Inc., Dillingham						X		
Whitney Fidalgo Seafoods, Inc., Naknek	X		X			X		
Alaska Marine Resources, Togiak							X	X

Source: Alaska, Department of Fish and Game, *Commercial Operators — 1972,*
Ststistical leaflet 24.

for the most part, is based on nonresident capital.[14]

Employment, Productivity, and Income

The employment impact of the fishing industry is significant, particularly with regard to the extreme seasonality of employment in the region. Rogers reports that for the period 1965 through 1970:

> ... 95 percent of the total annual man-months of employment were in the months of June and July, when the main red salmon runs materialize. On a weekly basis this concentration would be even more dramatic. Except for very minor catch of other species of lesser commercial value in May and extending into August, this is the total extent of annual employment for most fishermen.[15]

Unemployment is very high in the Bristol Bay region except during salmon season. The unemployment rate was estimated by the Alaska Department of Labor to be 26 percent during February 1970. This compared to a statewide average of 10 percent. The seasonal absence of employment opportunities can also be expressed as a ratio of employed people to the total population eighteen years old and older. In February 1970, this ratio was 43.5 percent in Bristol Bay compared with 69.4 percent for the state.[16]

Historically, nonresident fishermen have been more productive than their resident counterparts. In 1939, the nonresident catch per fisherman was 2.7 times as much as the resident catch, and in 1970, the nonresident catch was 2.1 times as much as the resident catch. Rogers argues that the observed difference in productivity can be attributed in part to the favored relationship that nonresidents have

---

[14]Gordon Scott Harrison, *Politics of Resource Development in Alaska: Primary Processing in the Salmon Industry*, ISEGR Occasional Papers No. 1, (Fairbanks: University of Alaska, Institute of Social, Economic and Government Research, July 1970).

[15]Rogers, *Labor Changes in Salmon Industry*, p. 56.

[16]Governor's Study Group, *A Limited Entry Program for Alaska's Fisheries*.

with the canneries.[17] An area biologist of the Department of Fish and Game familiar with Bristol Bay area has suggested that some of the difference in the comparative production of resident and nonresident fishermen can also be attributed to differences in motivation and objectives.

> *Most of the nonresident fishermen are high-liners, that is, they consistently make large catches and are able to do so due to better gear and boats than possessed by many resident fishermen. A nonresident who comes all the way up from outside is going to fish pretty hard. Many of these fishermen have fished Bristol Bay for many years. On the other hand, there are about three major groups of resident fishermen: (1) the high-liners, who consistently make good catches and can and do compete with the nonresident; (2) the part-time or weekend fisherman who cannot compete. Most of these vacation fishermen use either skiffs and/or older gear and vessels which cannot compete with the larger mobile high-liner fleet; (3) the last group of resident fishermen are the upriver Native fishermen—they largely cannot compete due to inadequate vessels. . . Further, these upriver fishermen have an entirely different approach to fishing as a livelihood. They normally catch just what they need to get through the next season.[18]*

A factor more directly responsible for the difference in productivity is that residents and nonresidents have generally employed different types of gear. The drift gill net, which is more productive than the set gill net, is used by a greater percentage of nonresidents. For the years 1970, 1972, and 1973, 89 percent of the nonresidents have been licensed for drift gill nets compared to 63 percent of the residents. For the period 1965-70, the average return per manmonth fishing effort for a drift gill net was 3,162 fish compared with 757 fish for a set net.

The gross receipts which have accrued to fishermen according to the type of gear used, regardless of residency, can be seen in Table 6-5. The average gross receipts per manmonth for the six-year period

---

[17]Rogers, *Labor Changes in Salmon Industry*, p. 57.

[18]Ibid.

Table 6-5
BRISTOL BAY REGION — GROSS RECEIPTS ACCRUING
TO FISHERMEN ACCORDING TO TYPE OF GEAR
1965-1970

| Year | Value to Fishermen per Man-Month* | |
	Drift Gill Nets	Set Gill Nets
1965	$ 6,169	$ 1,089
1966	2,527	724
1967	1,535	414
1968	1,312	401
1969	2,992	1,228
1970	6,385	1,265
Six year average	3,487	854

*Value is allocated to gear on basis of number of fish caught.
 Assumes same price was paid for drift and set net fish.

Source: George W. Rogers, "A Study of the Socio-Economic Impact of Changes
in the Harvesting Labor Force in the Alaska Salmon Industry," (University of
Alaska, Institute of Social, Economic and Government Research, December
1972) Table 21.

1965-70 was $3,487 for drift gill nets and $854 for set gill nets. Thus, the drift nets are, on the average, over four times as productive as the set nets.

Rogers has calculated the gross receipts according to residency and found that in 1970, the gross receipts per resident amounted to $3,871 and that nonresidents earned $8,415. It should be recalled that a much larger proportion of the nonresidents used drift nets than did the residents. Rogers also estimated the gross receipts and net income for resident and nonresident drift net vessel operators based on a sample of 455 resident and 319 nonresident tax returns for 1969. Gross receipts were calculated to be $4,660 for nonresidents and $3,871 for residents. After deducting operating costs, Rogers estimated the net return per resident fisherman to be $1,936 as compared to $2,149 for nonresidents. Thus, when the same gear is employed, the residents earn only 10 percent less than the nonresidents. This indicates that most, if not all, of the apparent difference in productivity is actually attributable to the different types of gear used by the two groups of fishermen.[19]

Foreign Fisheries Involvement in the Bristol Bay Area

There is direct competition between Japanese and U.S. fishermen for the Bristol Bay salmon resource. Although U.S. fishermen harvest all of the salmon in the Bristol Bay and Eastern Bering Sea areas, salmon of Bristol Bay origin are harvested outside this area by the Japanese fleet on the high seas west of 175 degrees W. longitude. Many of these salmon, if not caught by Japanese fishermen, would return to the Bristol Bay fishery. From 1950 through 1969, the Japanese high seas harvest of sockeye salmon east of 170 degrees E longitude accounted for only 11 percent of the total harvest for these years.[20] However, when North American runs are low, as has been the case in 1972 and 1973, this percentage is several times

[19] Ibid., pp. 38, 64-65.

[20] Eugene H. Buck, *National Patterns and Trends of Fishery Development in the North Pacific*, Anchorage: University of Alaska, Arctic Environmental Information and Data Center, 1973.

greater. In 1973, for example, 757 thousand sockeye salmon, which originated in Bristol Bay, were harvested by Bristol Bay fishermen and 630 thousand were taken by Japanese fishermen.[21] Thus in this low-run year, the Japanese catch equaled nearly half of the total Bristol Bay salmon harvest.

Table 6-6 shows the extent to which other nations harvest the fish resources of the waters adjacent to the Bristol Bay region. It also gives an idea of the type and to some extent the quantity of fish that could be harvested by U.S. fishermen if they should so choose. The waters adjacent to Bristol Bay coincide with the area known as the Eastern Bering Sea (see Map 6-2). It extends from Bristol Bay westward to 175 degrees West Longitude and northward from the Aleutians to the Bering Strait.

U.S. fishermen have provided very little competition for their foreign counterparts fishing in the Eastern Bering Sea, even for those species currently of economic importance in other parts of Alaska, such as shrimp, king crab, herring and halibut. From the beginning of the first recorded catch of each species through 1969, foreign fishermen harvested 90 percent of the king crab, 100 percent of the herring and about 44 percent of the halibut. More recently, however, the annual catch of king crab by U.S. fishermen has exceeded that of foreign fishermen in this area. Fish resources such as pollock and flatfish remain untouched by U.S. fishermen, although as of 1969, foreign fishermen had harvested an estimated 16 billion pounds of these species from the Eastern Bering Sea. Such results show that there is a good potential for diversifying the fishing industry in Bristol Bay. In fact, such diversification may be the only alternative for the economy of the area, if the salmon fishery continues to decline.

Subsistence Fishing, Hunting, and Trapping

Subsistence fishing accounts for an important part of the family

---

[21] ADF&G *Area Management Report, Bristol Bay, 1972* and Tom Schroeder, Fisheries Biologist, Alaska, Department of Fish and Game, Dillingham Office, personal interview, December 11, 1973.

Table 6-6

FOREIGN FISHERIES INVOLVEMENT IN BRISTOL BAY

Species	Year of First Recorded Catch	Total Historic Catch[a] (millions of pounds)	National Distribution of Catch (Approx. percentage)	
King Crab	1930	514.9	Japan	70
			USSR	20
			USA	10
Pollock	1933	6325.2[b]	Japan	92
			USSR	8
Pacific Cod	1905	743.4[c]	Japan	70
			USSR	30
Halibut	1905	112.7	USSR	44
			USA	24
			Canada	24
			Japan	8
Flatfish (excluding Halibut)	1933	5797.2[b]	Japan	70
			USSR	30
Salmon (all species)	1905	5098.7	USA	100

[a]From first recorded catch to 1969.

[b]Entire Eastern Bering Sea catch; Bristol Bay harvest would be less than 30 percent of this total.

[c]Entire Bering Sea catch; Bristol Bay harvest would be less than 10 percent of this total.

Source: Eugene H. Buck, *National Patterns and Trends of Fishery Development in the North Pacific*, University of Alaska, Arctic Environmental Information and Data Center, Anchorage: 1973.

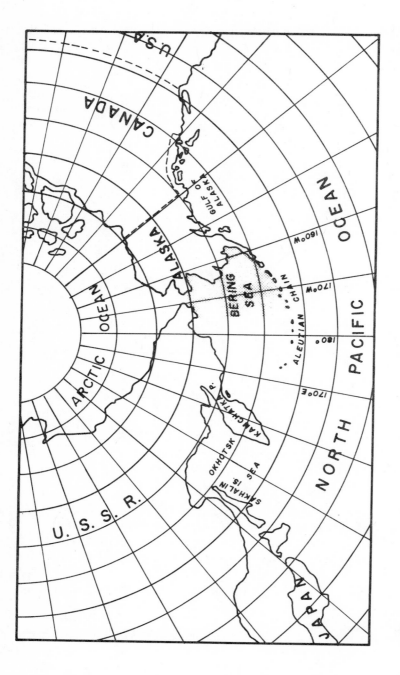

Map 6-2: Eastern Bering Sea Fishing Region

diet of residents of Bristol Bay, especially those living upriver or on the lakes. According to a recent study not yet released by The Alaska Department of Fish and Game, estimates of the yearly average subsistence catch for the years 1963 through 1973 are as follows:[22]

The 1971 area biologist's report describes the present Bristol Bay subsistence fishery as follows:

> Salmon subsistence catches for personal use and dog food consumption have been recorded since 1963 in Bristol Bay. This subsistence fishery is primarily centered around the Naknek-Kvichak and Nushagak drainages where local inhabitants, especially outlying villagers, still depend on salmon for winter dog food and augmentation to their own diets. Salmon subsistence catches in the two major drainages approach 130,000 to 170,000 fish annually.

> In the Togiak district, the only other area where considerable subsistence fishing takes place, main reliance is placed on sea-run char, which apparently winter in the Togiak River. From interviews with knowledgeable persons in the Togiak area, it is conservatively estimated that over 100,000 char are harvested annually from the Togiak River with small mesh gill nets between September and May. It is further estimated that between 5,000 to 10,000 salmon of all species are taken for subsistence purposes, almost all of which originate from the Togiak River drainage.

> Considerable winter fishing takes place through the ice in all districts of Bristol Bay. Winter catches consist primarily of arctic char, whitefish, pike, burbot and some rainbow and grayling. However, the large area involved and the sporadic fishing efforts have precluded efforts to monitor these catches.

> The 1971 subsistence salmon catch was over 120,000 fish of all species for the Naknek-Kvichak and Nushagak districts. Since 1963, the average subsistence salmon harvest for the two major districts has averaged 128,100 fish of all species, with over 56 percent coming from the Naknek-Kvichak area.[23]

---

[22]Alaska, Department of Fish and Game, unpublished statewide subsistence statistics.

[23]Rogers, *Labor Force Changes in Salmon Industry*, p. 58.

Annual subsistence records for the Naknek-Kvichak and the Nushagak districts show a relatively stable production for salmon subsistence regardless of the fluctuations of the commercial catch. From 1963 through 1971, the year-to-year variation in the subsistence catch averaged less than 10 percent. These fluctuations only slightly reflected the fluctuations in the commercial catch which were of a considerably greater magnitude. This indicates that subsistence fishing is primarily a function of resident need rather than the amount of fish available.

Hunting and trapping are not as important to the Bristol Bay economy as they were before the development of the commercial salmon fishery. Before the fishery was established, wildlife was the major source of food and clothing; cash was needed only to purchase supplies. After the industry was established, most Bristol Bay Natives began to earn incomes from fishing and no longer completely depended on subsistence activities. However, wildlife still remains an important food source as well as a supplementary source of money income. Trapping has declined, probably because of the declining price of furs and the scarcity of furbearers due to overtrapping in some parts of the region. The important furbearers trapped in the region include: beaver, muskrat, mink, land otter, and red fox. For the period 1958-1968, a yearly average of 1,500 beaver, 200 muskrat, 400 mink, 200 land otter, and 300 red fox were trapped.[24]

Moose and caribou are important sources of fresh meat in the Bristol Bay region. It was estimated by the Federal Field Committee that for the period 1958-1968, the yearly harvest of moose and caribou averaged 500 animals each. The total brown and black bear harvest for this period was about 225 animals per year, and along the coastal areas about 1,000 harbor seals were taken annually. The Federal Field Committee also estimated that 100,000 waterfowl were harvested yearly between 1958 and 1968.[25]

---

[24] Federal Field Committee for Development Planning in Alaska, *Alaska Natives and the Land*, Anchorage: 1968 (Available through Superintendent of Documents, Washington, D. C., 20402).

[25] Ibid.

Rogers has pointed out that the subsistence activities are quite economically valuable to those who engage in them because substitutes for the food supplied by subsistence activities would otherwise have to come from cash purchases requiring either increased wage employment, which is not available in the region, or welfare payments.[26]

Agriculture

Agriculture is practically nonexistent in the Bristol Bay region. There are no commercial feed crops or vegetables produced. There is, however, a small reindeer herd on Hagemeister Island which was started in 1965 with reindeer loaned from the BIA herd on Nunivak Island.[27] There are now 450 animals on Hagemeister Island grazing on federally leased land (see Map 6-3) and it is estimated that the island could support 1,000 reindeer. During 1973, some reindeer were harvested from the Hagemeister Island herd, processed at the cold storage plant in Togiak, and marketed locally.[28] Data on this reindeer operation is not yet available.

Minerals and Petroleum

There is no major mineral or petroleum production activity currently taking place in the Bristol Bay region, although considerable exploration (especially for oil) has occurred in the past. The Bristol Bay region makes up part of a large sedimentary basin which is considered to have a high potential for oil and gas development. Early in the century, unsuccessful attempts were made to locate oil south of Becharof Lake. More recently, two wells were drilled, plugged, and abandoned near Port Moller in 1963 and Ugashik in

---

[26]Rogers, *Labor Force Changes in Salmon Industry*, p. 59.

[27]U.S. Department of the Interior, Bureau of Indian Affairs, "Hagemeister Island, Alaska," unpublished, 1966.

[28]Joint Federal-State Land Use Planning Commission, Fact Sheets on D-2 areas —Hagemeister Island, Anchorage: 1973.

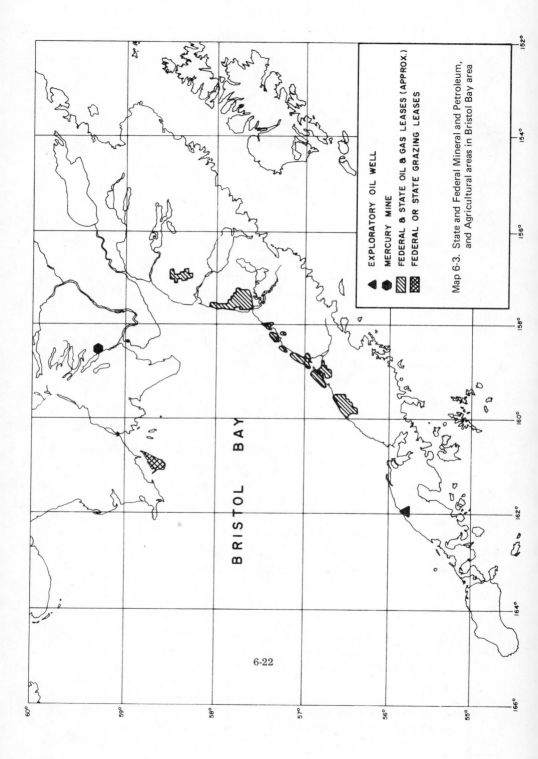

BRISTOL BAY

EXPLORATORY OIL WELL

MERCURY MINE

FEDERAL & STATE OIL & GAS LEASES (APPROX.)

FEDERAL OR STATE GRAZING LEASES

Map 6-3. State and Federal Mineral and Petroleum, and Agricultural areas in Bristol Bay area

6-22

1966.[29] During the late 1960's, extensive offshore exploration in the region was conducted by several oil companies. In 1968, the state of Alaska sponsored a competitive oil and gas lease sale for offshore tracts in the Bristol Bay area. The state offered to lease 350 thousand acres and ended up leasing 165 thousand acres at $18 per acre, which resulted in a total bonus to the state of about $3 million.[30] Federal onshore leases in the Bristol Bay area as of 1971 totaled about 640 thousand acres (Map 6-3).[31] Currently, an exploratory well is being drilled near the Bristol Bay area on the north shore of the Alaska Peninsula at Cape Leonivitch. The results of this drilling are not yet known.[32]

According to a listing of mining claims made by the Mineral Industry Research Laboratory at the University of Alaska, there are roughly 20 active and 130 inactive mining claims in the Bristol Bay area.[33] The most promising mine in the region is the mercury mine located 25 miles north of Dillingham near Marsh Mountain (see Map 6-3). This mine has been active off and on for the past several years. It is expected that the mine would become active again if the price of mercury should rise sufficiently to make the operation profitable.

Tourism and Recreation

Tourism and recreation are not major activities in the Bristol Bay region. Although available data are quite sketchy, it appears that

[29] ASHA, *Dillingham Comprehensive Plan*, June 1971, p. 47.

[30] Alaska, Department of Natural Resources, Division of Lands, *1972 Annual Report*, p. 5-13.

[31] Ibid., p. 48. ASHA Dillingham Comprehensive Plan, June 1971, p. 47.

[32] Thomas Marshall, Alaska, Department of Natural Resources, Division of Oil and Gas, telephone conversation, August 1973.

[33] Lawrence E. Heiner and Eve Porter, *A Computer Processable Storage and Retrieval Program for Alaska Mineral Information*, Report No. 24, Vol. 2, Fairbanks: University of Alaska, Mineral Industry Research Laboratory.

significant numbers of tourists visit only one area in the region: Katmai National Monument. The greater proportion of visitors to Katmai consist of tour groups and fishermen.[34] The National Monument is also used by military personnel from the King Salmon Air Force Base, researchers, backcountry users, and local residents. In 1972, a total of 16,700 people visited Katmai.[35]   No figures are available which would indicate what proportion of these were tourists.

In addition to Katmai National Monument, there are excellent opportunities for outdoor recreation activities of high enough quality and quantity to attract tourists both from within and from outside the state. The Iliamna Lake and Wood River-Tikchik Lake areas are famous for their trophy trout fishing and big game hunting. There are numerous hunting and fishing lodges and camps in the region, and nearly half of the state's registered guides are licensed to guide there.[36] No statistics are available which would show the amount of business done by the lodges or by the guides of the Bristol Bay area.

[34]Pamela Rich and Arlon R. Tussing, *The National Park System in Alaska—An Economic Impact Study* (Fairbanks: University of Alaska, Institute of Social, Economic and Government Research, 1973) p. 41.

[35]Alaska, Department of Natural Resources, Division of Parks, *Alaska Outdoor Recreation Historic Preservation* (1972) p. 35.

[36]U.S. Department of Commerce, Division of Occupational Licensing, *State of Alaska Guide Register*, Juneau: 1973.

Overview

The Bristol Bay region, one of the most isolated areas in Alaska, is essentially a mountain-bordered basin which opens away from the state's population centers and shipping lanes. It is not accessible by Alaska's overland highway, railroad, or marine highway systems. In addition, the area lacks deepwater ports; sea cargo must be lightered to shore. The shipping season, because of winter sea ice, lasts only from May to November. For these reasons, air transportation plays a key role in the transport system. Difficult access combined with a relatively low volume of freight and passenger traffic make transportation costs very high.

Transportation Facilities

Airports

Nearly every village in the region has airports or float plane landing sites. The many lakes and rivers provide adequate landing sites for float planes in summer and ski-equipped planes in winter.

The Bristol Bay area has nine trunk airports with runways 3,500 feet or longer that are capable of accomodating large aircraft. Five of these are lighted and can handle nighttime traffic. Jet aircraft regularly use the airports at Dillingham and King Salmon. However, only the King Salmon airport has a paved runway and facilities for plane handling, maintenance, and traffic control. The remaining airports and landing sites in the region are suitable for only small aircraft. They have runways shorter than 3,500 feet and are unlighted. There is a heliport located at the Alaska Native Service Hospital at Kanakanak. Statistics on the region's airports can be seen in Table 7-1.

Roads

The Bristol Bay region has approximately 103 miles of permanent roads and jeep trails. Six short, unconnected roads account for most of this mileage. Local service roads make up the remainder, such as those which connect some of the villages to their airports. Table 7-2 gives information concerning the length and type of these roads.

The Dillingham-Aleknagik road provides the residents of Aleknagik (which has no stores) access to one of the region's major distribution centers. Dillingham is also connected to the Alaska Native Service hospital at Kanakanak by road. Part of the supplies for Lake Iliamna communities are shipped over the Iliamna Portage Road that connects Lake Iliamna with Iliamna Bay. Approximately 450 tons of supplies and from 10 to 40 boats move over this Portage Road annually.[1] The road is very difficult to traverse and is closed in the winter. The Newhalen River road runs north from Newhalen on Lake Iliamna toward Lake Clark but stops short of the lake. The Katmai jeep trail is used only during the summer months by a concessionaire in Katmai National Monument who takes tourists from Brooks Camp on Lake Naknek to the Valley of Ten Thousand Smokes. The Naknek-King Salmon road connects the two largest towns of Bristol Bay Borough and receives heavy use in terms of freight shipped between Naknek harbor and King Salmon.

The State Highway Department plans to undertake small-scale construction and/or upgrading of the region's roads over the next five years. The estimated cost of these activities for the period 1973 through 1977 will be slightly over 7 million dollars (See Table 7-3). Preliminary engineering and/or right-of-way work is expected to commence within the 1973-77 period on the proposed trunk road between Iniskin Bay and King Salmon. The road will pass north of

---

[1] Alaska, Dept. of Highways, *Peninsula Crossing Study*, p. 39.

Table 7-1
AIRPORTS IN THE BRISTOL BAY AREA
1973

Location	Operator	Length (feet)	Width (feet)	Surface Type	Population Served[d]	Largest Aircraft[d]
Aleknagik	Private	1,400				
Aleknagik Mission	Private	1,200				
Bear Creek		1,600				
Big Mountain (L)[a]	Air Force	4,000				
Clarks Point	State	2,000		Gravel	171	
Dillingham		1,200				
Dillingham (old)		2,100				
Dillingham Mun. (L)[a]		5,000	150	Gravel	500	Boeing 737
Egegik	State	1,900	95	Gravel	148	
Ekuk		1,500		Silt		
Ekwok		2,200	80	Silt	103	Twin Otter
Igiugig	State	2,700	150	Sand and Gravel	36	
Iliamna (L)[a]	FAA	3000/5000[b]	200/160	Gravel and Silt	58	Fokker 27 & Hercules
Jensens		4,700				
Kakhonak	State	2000/1200[b]	100/100	Gravel	88	
King Salmon (L)[a-c]	FAA	8500/5000[b]	150/300	Asphalt	202	DC-8
King Salmon	None	Naknek River		Seadrome		
Koggiung	State	1,000	40	Sand		
Kulik Lake	Private	4,600	140	Sand and Gravel		
Kulik Lake	Private	Lake		Seadrome		

(continued on next page)

Table 7-1 (continued from previous page)

Location	Operator	Length (feet)	Width (feet)	Surface Type	Population Served[d]	Largest Aircraft[d]
Kvichak	Private	800/800[b]	50/50	Silt and Sand		
Levelock	State	1600/1500[b]	100/50	Silt	74	
Nakeen		1,300				
Naknek	State	1,700	90	Silt	178	Cessna 180
New Stuyahok		1,500		Silt		
Nondalton	State	2,225	100	Gravel	74	
Nushagak		2,500				
Painter Creek	Private	5,000	150	Gravel		
Pedro Bay	State	1,600	50	Sand	65	
Pilot Point	State	1,860	50	Silt and Gravel	68	Grumman Goose
Port Alsworth		2,500				
Port Heiden (L)[a]		7,500	300		66	
South Naknek	None	1,350	75	Silt	154	
Togiak		3,500		Silt and Gravel		
Ugashik	None	1,245	65	Silt		

[a] (L) denotes lighting facilities available

[b] Two runways

[c] King Salmon FAA facility also provides controlled approach systems and direction finding station

[d] Where data is available

Sources: A Limited Entry Program for Alaska's Fisheries, Governor's Study Group on Limited Entry, State of Alaska, Juneau 1973.

Alaska, Department of Public Works, Division of Aviation — Landing Area Inventory — 1973 (prepared for the Joint Federal—State Land Use Planning Commission.

Alaska, Department of Highways, Peninsula Crossing — Socio-Economic Study, 1969.

Table 7-2
PERMANENT ROADS
BRISTOL BAY REGION 1973

Name	Length (miles)	Width (feet)	Type
Dillingham-Aleknagik Road and Kanakanak Spur	26.1	18	Graded and drained
Iliamna Portage Road	15.5	10	Graded and drained
Katmai Jeep Trail	20.0	10	Unimproved
King Salmon AFB - Fishing Camps Road	8.0	14	Graded and drained
Naknek-King Salmon Road	15.5	24	Graded and drained
Newhalen River Road	18.0	18	Unimproved
Total	103.1		

Sources: Alaska, Department of Highways, General Highway Maps, Dillingham, Illiamna and Naknek Quadrangles.

Alaska, Department of Highways, *Peninsula Crossing — Socio-Economic Study, 1969.*

Table 7-3
PROPOSED HIGHWAY AND SERVICE ROAD
CONSTRUCTION ACTIVITIES FOR BRISTOL BAY
1973-1977

Project Location	Project Description	Estimated Total Cost (Dollars)
	(1) Construction and Improvement of Major Roads	
	1973—None	
	1974—None	
Dillingham — Kanakanak	1975—Reconstruction and new construction and pave 5.7 miles	2,610,000
Naknek— King Salmon	1976—Pave 15.5 miles on existing alignment	2,040,000
Newhalen— Nondalton	1977—Reconstruction and new construction and gravel surface 22.3 miles including construction of one bridge	2,385,000
Subtotal		7,035,000
	(2) Preliminary engineering and/or right of way work expected to commence within this five-year program on the following projects:	
Alaska Peninsula Crossing	Kamishak Bay to Naknek	
	Construction and Improvement of Local and Service Roads	

(continued on next page)

Table 7-3 (continued from previous page)

Project Location	Project Description	Estimated Total Cost (Dollars)
Bristol Bay Borough	1973—Construct various Borough roads	20,000
New Koliganek	Reconstruct various village streets	*
Dillingham	1974—Reconstruct 1st Avenue and "D" Street	*
Ekwok	Reconstruct access road from village to airport	*
Twin Hills	Construct access road from village to airport	*
Bristol Bay Borough	1975—Reconstruct various borough roads	20,000
	1976 and 1977—None planned to date.	
Total		7,075,000

*Specific cost information not available.

Source: Alaska, Department of Highways, *Five-Year Highway Construction Program — 1972.*

Lake Iliamna and will be approximately 180 miles long. The construction plans and timing for this road are not yet definite. In 1968 it was estimated that the road would cost approximately 29 million dollars.[2]

Harbors

Harbor facilities in the Bristol Bay area are limited by the complete lack of deepwater ports. Deep draft vessels must unload their cargo into smaller boats as much as six miles from shore and lighter it into the region's ports.[3] The majority of the harbor facilities are owned and operated by fish processing plants. Some of the harbors have equipment to haul boats out of the water and make minor repairs, and some can provide supplies such as food and marine hardware. Fresh water is available at practically all of the harbors. Information concerning the facilities and supplies available at each harbor in the region is provided in Table 7-4.

· Transportation Services

Passenger Service

Virtually all of the passenger traffic into and out of the Bristol Bay area is by air. Three certificated route carriers—Kodiak Western Alaska Airlines, Wien Air Alaska, Inc., and Reeve Aleutian Airways—serve the region along with nine air-taxi operators. Certified air carrier routes for the region can be seen on Map 7-1. Approximately 80 percent of the villages listed in the U.S. Census receive scheduled commercial air service at least once a week, and most of these receive scheduled service three or more times a week (See Table 7-5). King Salmon has daily flight connections with Anchorage, and there are flights between Dillingham and Anchorage

---

[2]Alaska, Department of Highways *Peninsula Crossing—Socioeconomic Study*, 1969.

[3]U.S. Department of commerce, Coast and Geodetic Survey, *United States Coast Pilot 9-Pacific and Arctic coasts, Alaska*, Seventh (1964) Edition, including 1966 and 1971 supplements.

Table 7-4
HARBOR FACILITIES
BRISTOL BAY

Harbor	Description
Pilot Point	Cannery-owned dock with 144-foot face which dries at low tide; fresh water available. Cannery facilities include: fuel storage tanks, machine shop, four ton crane and scowway.
Ugashik	Cannery-owned wharf with 200-foot face which dries at half tide. Cannery facilities include: fuel storage tanks, machine shop, two-ton crane and scowway.
Egegik	Cannery-owned wharf with 150-foot and 80-foot faces which dry at low tide. Fresh water, food staples and clothing available; marine railway and five ton crane.
Naknek	Numerous cannery docks; large fuel tank farm and tidal dock belonging to Standard Oil; some supplies available at canneries; boat repair service provided by canneries only for baits that fish for them.
Igiugig	Numerous cannery wharves, the longest of which is 450 feet. All are dry at low tide. Fresh water is available. Marine railway at 450-foot dock can haul out vessels up to 160 tons.
Ekuk	Cannery wharf with 150-foot face; cannery facilities include fuel storage tanks, fresh water and marine railway with a 60-ton capacity.
Clarks Point	Cannery wharf with 175-foot face; cannery facilities include: general store, fuel storage tanks, a marine railway with 150-ton capacity, and a small machine shop. Fresh water is available.
Dillingham	Cannery wharf with 178-foot face; cannery facilities include fuel storage tanks and a marine railway with 100-ton capacity.

Sources: U.S. Department of Commerce, Coast and Geodetic Survey, United States Coast Pilot 9 — Pacific and Arctic Coasts, Alaska, Seventh Edition, including 1966 and 1971 supplements, 1964; B.J. Logan, marine insurance adjuster, Anchorage, unpublished notes, 1973.

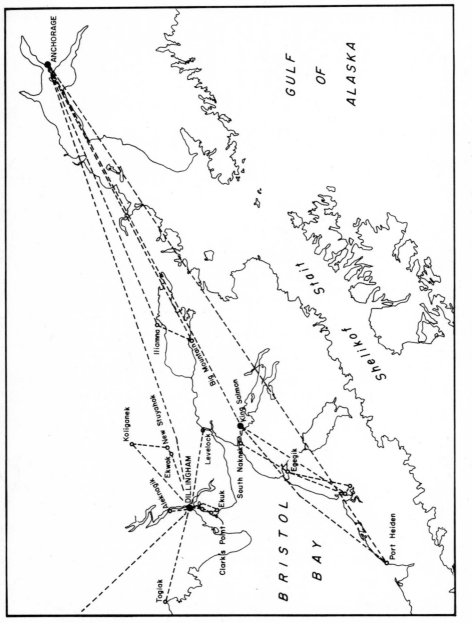

Map 7-1: Certified Air Carrier Routes for Bristol Bay Area

Table No. 7-5
NON-STOP AIRLINE FLIGHTS
BRISTOL BAY, AUGUST 1973

To:	From:	Flights per week	Flight time (minutes)	One-way fare	Type of Aircraft*
Aleknagik	Dillingham	3	15	$ 11	PRP
Anchorage	Big Mountain	3	65	38	F27
Anchorage	Dillingham	7	90	55	F27
Anchorage	King Salmon	7	55	46	737
Anchorage	Port Heiden	2	100	87	Y11
Bethel	Dillingham	1	80	28	PRP
Big Mountain	Iliamna	3	15	7	F27
Clarks Point	Queen Fisheries	14	15	6	PRP
Dillingham	Aleknagik	3	30	11	PRP
Dillingham	Anchorage	7	90	55	F27
Dillingham	Bethel	1	85	28	PRP
Dillingham	Ekuk	14	25	11	PRP
Dillingham	King Salmon	7	25	18	F27
Dillingham	King Salmon	5	35	22	PRP
Dillingham	Koliganek	5	55	22	PRP
Dillingham	Levelock	3	60	17	PRP
Dillingham	New Stuyahok	10	85	17	PRP
Dillingham	South Naknek	7	35		PRP
Dillingham	Togiak	12	55	22	PRP
Dillingham	Pilot Point	13	20	14	PRP
Egegik	Ugashik	1	45	14	PRP

(continued on next page)

7-11

Table 7-5)continued from previous page)

To:	From:	Flights per week	Flight time (minutes)	One-way fare	Type of Aircraft*
Ekuk	Clarks Point	14	15	6	PRP
Ekwok	Dillingham	15	20	14	PRP
Igiugig	King Salmon	2	30	22	PRP
Iliamna	Anchorage	3	65	35	F27
King Salmon	Anchoraqe	7	55	46	737
King Salmon	Dillingham	7	25	18	F27
King Salmon	Dillingham	8	35	22	PRP
King Salmon	Igiugig	2	45	22	PRP
King Salmon	South Naknek	35	20	10	PRP
Koliganek	New Stuyahok	5	30	11	PRP
Levelock	King Salmon	3	20	12	PRP
New Stuyahok	Ekwok	15	25	6	PRP
Pilot Point	King Salmon	14	70	27	PRP
Port Heiden	Ivanoff Bay	2	100	35	PRP
Port Heiden	King Salmon	3	45	42	Y11
Port Heiden	Sand Point	2	100	44	Y11
Queen Fisheries	Dillingham	14	10	11	PRP
South Naknek	Dillingham	7	30		PRP
South Naknek	Egegik	14	30		PRP
South Naknek	King Salmon	21	10	10	PRP
Togiak	Dillingham	12	40	22	PRP
Ugashik	Pilot Point	1	5	6	PRP

* PRP = Prop Aircraft, type varies
  F27 = Fokkor Friendship Turbo-Prop F27
  737 = Boeing 737
  Y11 = Namco YS-11

Source: Official Air Freight Local Rates Tariff, No. LR-1, Reeve Aleutian Airways, Inc.; Wien Air Alaska; Western Airlines, August 15, 1973.

every day except Sunday (Table 7-5).[4]

Dillingham and King Salmon are by far the region's busiest airports (Table 7-6). In FY 1971, the number of passengers enplaning at Dillingham totaled 12,611 or 40 percent of the region's total commercial enplanements. King Salmon accounted for 42 percent of the region's enplanements, with 13,250 passengers. Between 1963 and 1971, the total yearly enplanements at Dillingham increased by 102 percent. The increase at King Salmon was 138 percent (Table 7-7).

Air taxi passenger activity in the region is also significant. According to statistics for 1972 compiled by the Alaska Transportation Commission, authorized air taxi operators in the area carried over 28,000 passengers (see Table 7-8). Thus, the air taxis carried at least as many passengers as the commercial airlines.

Freight Service

The bulk of the air freight and mail for the region is carried by certificated air route carriers. Only one air taxi operator carried U.S. mail in 1971. Villages receiving scheduled air passenger service receive air freight service on a regular basis, but it is often delayed.

Almost all of the air freight in the region passed either through Dillingham or King Salmon airports. However, statistics are only available for the amount of freight shipped out of each airport and not the quantities received by these facilities. Of the cargo transported by commercial carriers, the Dillingham airport shipped out 850 tons of freight and mail in FY 1971, and the King Salmon airport shipped out 670 tons (see Tables 7-6 and 7-7). The output of the two airports accounted for 93 percent of the commercial cargo in the region. Between 1963 and 1971, the amount of air freight and mail shipped out of the Dillingham Airport by commercial carriers increased by 236 and 292 percent, respectively. The amount of air freight and mail sent out of the King Salmon Airport for the same

---

[4]Some of these flights have been affected by the energy crisis.

Table 7-6
AIRPORT* ACTIVITY STATISTICS
OF CERTIFICATED ROUTE AIR CARRIERS
BRISTOL BAY, F.Y. 1971

Airport	Passengers	Shipped out		Total Cargo & Mail (tons)
		Freight (tons)	Mail (tons)	
Aleknagik	124	0.65	6.56	7.21
Clarks Point	219	3.60	5.12	8.72
Dillingham	12,611	417.06	432.09	849.15
Egegik	382	4.34	7.47	11.81
Ekuk	603	3.54	1.68	5.22
Ekwok	568	0.25	1.76	2.01
Igiugig	38	0.09	0.18	0.27
Iliamna	673	13.30	9.11	22.24
King Salmon	13,280	405.65	263.85	669.50
Levelock	376	0.14	2.00	2.14
Manokotak	541	4.52	3.59	8.11
New Stuyahok	594	0.81	3.44	4.25
Pilot Point	166	0.22	3.06	3.28
Port Heiden	293	19.08	14.70	33.78
South Naknek	41	0.11	0.29	0.40
Togiak	1,448	3.69	8.95	12.64
Ugashik	110	0.03	12.14	12.17
Totals	32,107	877.08	775.99	1,652.70

* Principal airports only

Source: U.S. Department of Transportation, Federal Aviation Agency, Civil
Aeronautics Board, *Airport Activity Statistics*, FY 1971.

Table 7-7

AIRPORT ACTIVITY STATISTICS – CERTIFICATED AIR ROUTE CARRIERS

BRISTOL BAY F.Y. 1963, 1966, 1972

Dillingham	Enplanements		
	Passengers	Freight (tons)	Mail (tons)
1963	6,238	124	110
1966	7,853	185	165
1971	12,611	417	432
Percent Increase 1963-1971	102	236	292
King Salmon			
1963	5,585	160	115
1966	9,673	185	163
1971	13,280	406	264
Percent Increase 1963-1971	138	153	130

Source: U.S. Department of Transportation, Federal Aviation Agency, Civil
Aeronautics Board, *Airport Activity Statistics, FY 1963, 1966, 1971.*

Table 7-8
AIR TAXI ACTIVITY
BRISTOL BAY 1972

Location of Operators	Total Passengers Carried	Tons of Freight Carried	Tons of U.S. Mail Carried	Total Tons Freight and Mail
Dillingham	4,981	20.7	—	20.7
King Salmon	11,226	156.6	69.3	225.9
Naknek—So. Naknek	12,215	10.2	—	10.2
Total	28,422	187.5	69.3	256.8

Source: Alaska Transportation Comission, Air Taxi Statistics, 1972 (office records).

period increased by 153 and 130 percent, respectively. Air taxi operators carried a total of 257 tons of freight and mail between airports in the region in 1972 (see Table 7-8).

As shown in Table 7-6, mail accounts for nearly half of all the air cargo carried in the region. Since all mail to rural Alaska goes by air regardless of whether it is airmail or surface parcel post, those goods that fall within parcel post size and weight limits can be shipped by air at the lower parcel post rate. Shippers use the U.S. Postal Service as a major freight mover in rural Alaska.[5]

Freight service by sea to the region is infrequent and unscheduled. The area is serviced by tug and barge approximately three times per year. Northstar III, the Bureau of Indian Affairs freighter, will visit some villages in the area upon request, usually once a year. Charter barge service is available from Anchorage or Seattle to haul large quantities of freight. The Legislative Affairs Agency reports that there is general dissatisfaction throughout rural Alaska with present tug and barge service from Seattle.[6] It cites the following complaints from rural Alaskans:

- High costs of both ocean freight and lighterage.

- Excessive damage of cargo.

- Undependable delivery.

- Lack of refrigeration service.

- Slow settlement of loss or damage claims.

- All freight must be prepaid to Alaska destinations.

---

[5] Alaska Legislative Council, Legislative Affairs Agency, *Transportation in Rural Alaska*, December 1972, pp. 5-8.

[6] Ibid., p. 9.

The principal harbors in Bristol Bay are Dillingham and Naknek. Table 7-9 shows the quantity of freight traffic moving through the two harbors. Naknek handled an average of about 55 thousand tons of cargo per year from 1961 through 1971. The average for Dillingham for the same period has been about 12 thousand tons. The majority of the freight shipped through both harbors is composed of three items: fuel oil, gasoline, and outbound fish and fish products. The yearly fluctuations in tonnage are mostly due to the fluctuations in outbound fish and fish products which vary according to the year's catch.

Freight deposited at Naknek is either transshipped to King Salmon by barge or other shallow draft boat via the Naknek River or by truck by way of the Naknek-King Salmon Road. During high water, freight can be shipped by launch to Lake Iliamna communities via the Kvichak River. The freight going to Aleknagik is carried from Dillingham by truck or is shipped by boat via the Wood River. Nushagak River communitiies within about 100 river miles of Dillingham have freight shipped up the river by launch.

Transportation Costs

One-way commercial airline passenger fares for some of the direct flights within the region and flights between Bristol Bay communities and Anchorage are shown in Table 7-5. In general, the passenger cost per mile tends to be higher in Alaska than for comparable distances in the contiguous United States, because of the lower traffic volume and higher operation and maintenance costs in Alaska (see Table 7-10).

Air freight rates for general commodities and selected items between Bristol Bay communities and Seattle are shown in Table 7-11. These rates are considerably higher than the rates for the same items between Anchorage and Seattle even when the extra distance is taken into account. Rates from Seattle to Iliamna or King Salmon are over a third higher than rates to Anchorage, while the distance is only 15 percent greater. Compared to the rates from Seattle to Anchorage, costs to Dillingham are about 50 percent higher. The average rates for southbound canned seafood to Seattle, when

Table 7-9
FREIGHT TRAFFIC MOVING
THROUGH BRISTOL BAY PORTS
1961-1971

	Tons of Freight Received, Shipped or Transferred	
Year	Naknek	Dillingham
1961	65,145	8,181
1962	31,858	15,368
1963	15,183	6,085
1964	60,679	7,479
1965	79,564	13,975
1966	44,074	17,332
1967	34,566	10,006
1968	18,920	6,896
1969	34,889	12,427
1970	149,339*	19,996
1971	68,554	10,079
Average/year	54,797	11,620

*Includes 64,160 tons of liquified

Source: U.S. Army Corps of Engineers, *Waterbourne Commerce of the United States*, 1961-1972.

Table 7-10
COMMERCIAL AIRLINE FARES
WITHIN BRISTOL BAY AND
BETWEEN BRISTOL BAY AND ANCHORAGE

Fare	Tourist One-way Fare (tax included)	Distance	Cost per Mile[*] (cents)
Anchorage—Dillingham	$55.00	330 mi.	.17
Anchorage—King Salmon	46.00	292	.16
Dillingham—King Salmon	18.00	67	.27
Port Heiden—King Salmon	42.00	140	.30

[*]Cost per mile computed from direct distance between points and tourist fare as of Sept. 1, 1973.

Source: *Official Airline Guide* (North American Edition), Oak Brook, Illinois: Reuben H. Donnelley Corporation Sept. 1, 1973.

Table 7-11

COMPARATIVE GENERAL AND SPECIFIC COMMODITY AIR FREIGHT RATES
BETWEEN SEATTLE and COMMUNITIES
OF THE BRISTOL BAY REGION
(dollars per 100 lbs)

From Seattle	To Anchorage	To Iliamna	To King Salmon	To Dillingham
General Commodities	$22.10	$28.40	$29.10	$32.65
Meat	19.20	25.50	24.20	29.75
Milk	16.90	23.20	23.90	27.45
Eggs	22.10	28.40	29.10	32.65
Produce	19.20	25.50	26.20	29.75
Household Goods	22.10	28.40	29.10	32.65
Personal Effects	22.10	28.40	29.10	32.65

To Seattle	From Anchorage	From Iliamna	From King Salmon	From Dillingham
Fresh Frozen Seafood	12.00	17.50	17.60	18.30
Canned Seafood	10.20	15.70	17.20	19.20

Source: Official Air Freight Local Rates Tariff, No. LR-1, Reeve Aleutian Airways, Inc.: Wien Air Alaska; Western Airlines.

compared to the rates from Anchorage, are roughly 50 percent higher from Iliamna, 70 percent higher from King Salmon, and 90 percent higher from Dillingham.

Sea freight rates to Bristol Bay communities are substantially higher than rates to other communities in the southwestern corner of Alaska. The higher costs are attributable to several factors: the greater distances involved, lighterage costs, difficult shipping conditions, and low freight volumes. Rates to Bristol Bay are approximately double the rates to Kodiak (see Table 7-12). A part of this difference is due to the lighterage costs which are about $0.63 per hundredweight in Bristol Bay.[7] Most of the cost difference, however, results from distance, shipping conditions, and low volume, and cannot be alleviated by improvements in harbor facilities.

----

[7] U.S. Department of the Interior, Bureau of Indian Affairs, Tariff 3, Lighterage and Longshoring Rates, Seattle: 1973.

Table No. 7-12
COMPARATIVE SEA FREIGHT RATES
(Cost per hundredweight)

From Seattle	To Kodiak	To Bristol Bay (Lighterage included)*
Cement, sand, gravel	$ 1.70	$ 4.19
Building woodwork	8.34	15.29
Metal collapsed cans in package	2.20	4.49
Fruits, vegetables -- frozen	7.92	14.57
Motor vehicles	8.51	14.58
Iron and steel articles	3.01	6.28
Lumber, rough or surfaced (strapped in bundles)	2.62	5.02
Eggs (in wooden cases)	4.66	8.59
Meat, fresh (not frozen)	8.21	19.47
Compressed gases	3.17	5.97
Salt	2.32	4.34
Fish canned (southbound)	2.32	4.88

*$0.63 per hundredweight (from Bureau of Indian Affairs Tariff No. 3)

Source: Sea Land Services, Inc., Tariff Nos. 130 and 197.

CHAPTER 8
LAND USE AND LAND STATUS[1]

Background Information

This discussion will include all the land encompassed by the Bristol Bay Native Corporation with the exception of the land which drains southward into the Western Gulf of Alaska. This southward draining land area will not be considered, because it pertains to the Western Gulf of Alaska geographically and has stronger economic ties with that area than with the Bristol Bay region.

The Bristol Bay region is currently undergoing a redistribution of land under the provisions of both the Alaska Statehood Act[2] and the Alaska Native Claims Settlement Act (ANCSA).[3] Until the final implementation of both acts, land ownership patterns and the uses permitted on the land will be changing constantly. These Acts will eventually produce three major landowners in the region: the federal government, the state and its municipalities, and the Alaska Natives. The Alaska Statehood Act passed in 1959 provided a grant of federal lands to the state amounting to 104.6 million acres. These lands are to be selected by the state from any open, available public domain lands owned by the United States. The state has selection rights until January 1984. State land selections in Bristol Bay are shown on Map 8-1.

---

[1] Information contained in this chapter is based upon the lands situation as of September 1, 1973.

[2] Alaska Public Law 85-508 (1958) 72 Stat. 339, Section 6.

[3] Alaska Public Law 92-204, Sections 11-22.

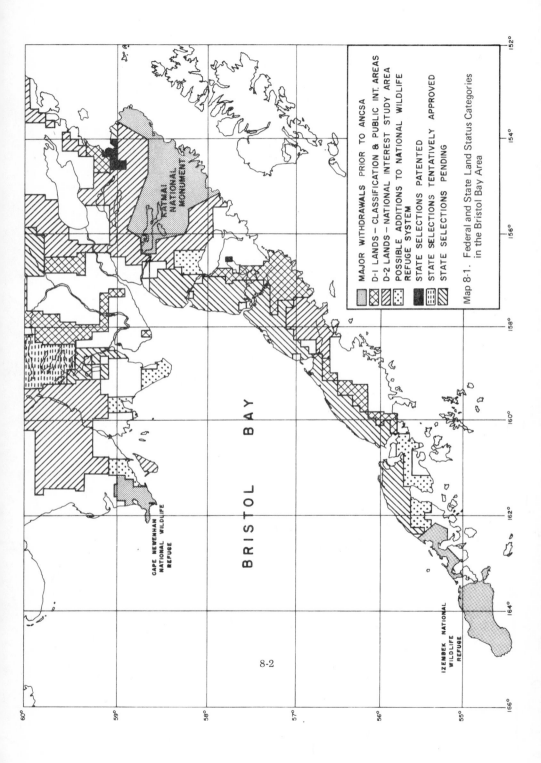

MAJOR WITHDRAWALS PRIOR TO ANCSA

D-I LANDS – CLASSIFICATION & PUBLIC INT. AREAS

D-2 LANDS – NATIONAL INTEREST STUDY AREA

POSSIBLE ADDITIONS TO NATIONAL WILDLIFE
REFUGE SYSTEM

STATE SELECTIONS PATENTED

STATE SELECTIONS TENTATIVELY APPROVED

STATE SELECTIONS PENDING

Map 8-1. Federal and State Land Status Categories
in the Bristol Bay Area

BRISTOL BAY

KATMAI NATIONAL MONUMENT

CAPE NEWENHAM NATIONAL WILDLIFE REFUGE

IZEMBEK NATIONAL WILDLIFE REFUGE

ANCSA, passed in 1971, provides for selection and conveyance of 40 million acres of Alaska to Alaska Natives and provides for the redistribution of most of the state's lands. The provisions of the act have priority over the land selection provisions in the Alaska Statehood Act. Because of this priority, state selection rights have been nullified on some lands and delayed on others. Under provisions of ANCSA, the Secretary of the Interior has withdrawn from the jurisdiction of the public land laws most of the public domain lands of Alaska. For the state as a whole, these withdrawals include:

- Approximately 106 million acres from which the Natives of Alaska can select their 40-million-acre entitlement.

- 7.5 million acres for utility corridors.

- 1.9 million acres for possible additions to the National Wildlife Refuge System.

- 80 million acres of lands of significant national importance to merit classification as a national forest, park, wild or scenic river or wildlife refuge (D-2 lands).

- 76 million acres of lands of significant public interest to warrant future classification by the Secretary of the Interior (D-1 lands).[4]

Except for utility corridor withdrawals, all of these categories of lands are represented in the Bristol Bay region and are shown on Maps 8-1 and 8-2.

Current Land Use

The economy of the Bristol Bay region is based primarily on the resources of the sea. Intensive use of the land occurs only where the land is used for a community or military site. Currently there are no

---

[4]Public Law 92-203 (Sec. 11), Public Land Orders: 5150, 5169, 5178, 5179, 5180, 5181, 5182, 5190, 5192, 5193, and reference (9).

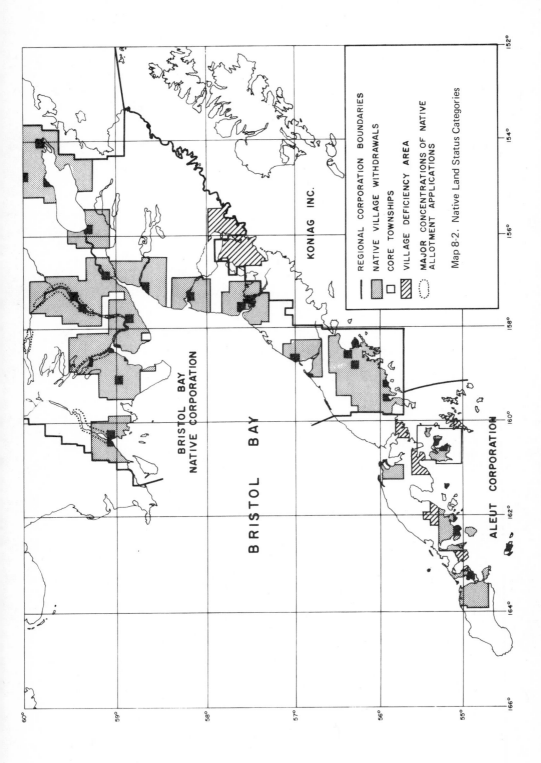

REGIONAL CORPORATION BOUNDARIES

NATIVE VILLAGE WITHDRAWALS

CORE TOWNSHIPS

VILLAGE DEFICIENCY AREA

MAJOR CONCENTRATIONS OF NATIVE
ALLOTMENT APPLICATIONS

Map 8-2. Native Land Status Categories

KONIAG INC.

BRISTOL BAY
NATIVE CORPORATION

BRISTOL BAY

ALEUT CORPORATION

other intensive uses of the land resources in the Bristol Bay area. Residents, however, extensively use the land area of the region for subsistence and recreational activities. Subsistence activities on the land primarily consist of hunting for moose and caribou and trapping for beaver, muskrat, mink, and red fox. Residents particularly seek fur bearers as a source of income when the salmon runs are low.[5] Very little information is available concerning the specific subsistence areas used by the residents of the region, nor are records available which show the numbers of animals harvested for subsistence purposes.

Recreational use of the Bristol Bay region centers around hunting, fishing, and sightseeing. Lake Iliamna attracts many trout fishermen to its trophy rainbow trout fishery. There are about fifty hunting and fishing lodges in the Bristol Bay region. The majority of these are in the Lake Iliamna area.[6] The areas adjacent to the lake and Katmai National Monument are popular with brown bear and moose hunters. Katmai National Monument is the major sightseeing attraction in the region.

Archeological sites represent another type of land use. The approximate location of these sites can be seen on Map 8-3. State Archeologist Dr. Karen Workman estimates that probably only half of the sites in the area have been discovered.[7] She feels this is especially true for the coastal areas which archeologists believe supported greater human populations in the past than in the present, because of the more reliable food supply provided by the sea. Many sites exist around Lake Iliamna; along the Naknek, Newhalen, and Kvichak Rivers; and at Dillingham. The Iliamna area is quite important for determining the Eskimo-Athabascan boundaries and the con-

---

[5] *Alaska Natives and the Land*, p. 303.

[6] Jay Hammond, Bristol Bay Borough, personal communication, February 20, 1973.

[7] Karen Workman, Archeologist, State of Alaska, Department of Natural Resources, Division on Parks, personal interview, August 29, 1973.

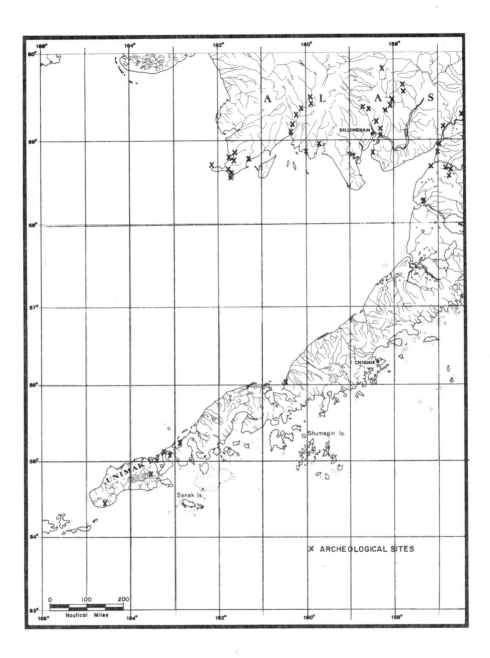

Map 8-3: Archeological Sites in Bristol Bay Area

tact between these ethnic groups. Archeologists have uncovered in Dillingham evidence of human occupation which spans 6,000 years, and they are just now realizing its archeological potential. Archeological finds on the Naknek River drainage show a possible span of over 4,000 years of human occupation.[8]

The Bristol Bay region contains approximately 24 million acres on which has been imposed fifteen land categories.[9] Some of these categories represent a permanent determination of land status; others have an indefinite status, while the remaining categories are of a temporary nature. The total area claimed for the different categories exceeds the actual area of the region by about 5 million acres. This has occurred because the ANCSA withdrawals overlap some of the previously withdrawn federal lands and lands previously selected by the state in accordance with the provisions of the Statehood Act. In addition, some of the Native village withdrawals overlap one another. A discussion of each land category, including the present status and the use limitations, follows. The land-use limitations in each category can be seen in Tables 8-1, 8-2, and 8-3.

Permanently Classified Lands

Lands in the Bristol Bay region which, because of the nature of their withdrawal, have permanent status include: Katmai National Monument, outer continental shelf lands, and state-patented and private-patented lands. Lands within Katmai National Monument and state-patented lands are shown on Map 8-1. Acreages for all categories except continental shelf lands are given in Table 8-4.

---

[8] Joint Federal-State Land Use Planning Commission for Alaska, *Hagemeister Island and Togiak*, April 1973. Joint Federal-State Land Use Planning Commission for Alaska, *Katmai Area, A Description*, April 1973.

[9] This figure was obtained by subtracting the acreage of the Bristol Bay regional corporation which drains into the Western Gulf of Alaska. These average estimates were obtained from the Bureau of Land Management computer printout of the Bristol Bay regional corporation.

Table 8-1

CONSTRAINTS TO USE ON LANDS WITHDRAWN UNDER ANCSA
AND REVOKED INDIAN RESERVE LANDS

Expiration Date:	D-2 Lands 12/18/78	Village Withdrawals 12/18/78	Village Deficiency Withdrawals 12/18/78	Regional Deficiency Withdrawals 12/18/78	D-1 and Classification Lands Indefinite	Wildlife Refuge Replacement Lands Indefinite
Appropriation Under Public Land Laws	No	No	No	No	No	No
Location and Entry Under Mining Laws	No	No	No	No	For metaliferous minerals only	No
Leasing under Minerals Leasing Act of 1920	No	No	No	No	No	No
Hunting, fishing and other forms of recreational use	Yes	Yes	Yes	Yes	Yes	Yes
Grazing	Yes*	Yes*	Yes*	Yes*	Yes*	Yes*
Timber Harvesting	Yes*	Yes*	Yes*	Yes*	Yes*	Yes*

a Provisions for interim administration in Section 17 of ANCSA authorize the Secretary of the Interior to make contracts and to grant leases, permits or easements on these lands. Under Present Bureau of Land Management policy this authority is rarely exercised and very few uses are permitted on the land.

Sources: Public Law 92-302 (ANCSA); Public Land Orders 5169 through 5188.

Table 8-2

CONSTRAINTS TO USE ON LANDS WITHDRAWN
PRIOR TO ANCSA AND
PENDING STATE SELECTIONS

	Katmai National Monument	Military Reservations	Power Sites or Projects	Outer Continental Shelf	Pending State Selections
Appropriation Under Public Land Laws	No	No	No	No	No
Location and Entry Under Mining Laws	No	No	Yes	No	No
Leasing Under Minerals Leasing Act of 1920	No	No	Yes	Yes	No
Hunting, Fishing, and Other Forms of Recreational Use	Yes (No Hunting)	Yes	Yes	N/A	Yes
Grazing	No	Yes	Yes	N/A	Yes*
Timber harvesting	No	Yes	Yes	N/A	Yes*

* The Secretary of the Interior has interim administrative authority on these lands giving him the right to make contracts and to grant leases or easements on these lands.

Source: Public Law 92-203 (ANCSA); Public Land Orders 5169 through 5188.

Table 8-3

LAND USE CONSTRAINTS GOVERNING LAND UNDER THE
JURISDICTION OF THE STATE OF ALASKA

Classification	Disposal	Mineral Deposits Acquired	Disposal of Timber and/or Materials	Grazing	Recreation
Unclassified lands	no	claim staking	no	no	yes
Agricultural lands	lease or sale	leasing	yes	short term lease	yes
Commercial lands	lease or sale	leasing	yes	short term lease	
Grazing lands	lease only	claim staking	yes	yes	yes
Industrial lands	lease or sale	leasing	yes	short term lease	yes
Material lands	no	claim staking	yes	yes	yes
Mineral lands	no*	claim staking	yes	yes	yes
Public recreation lands	no	leasing	yes	no	yes
Private recreation lands	lease or sale	leasing	yes	short term lease	yes
Residential lands	lease or sale	leasing	yes	short term lease	yes
Reserved use lands	no	leasing	yes	no	yes
Timber lands	no	claim staking	yes	yes	yes
Utility lands	lease or sale	claim staking	yes	short term lease	yes
Watershed lands	no		yes	yes	yes
Open-to-entry lands	lease or sale	leasing	yes	no	yes
Tidal and submerged lands	lease or sale	leasing	yes	NA	yes

*Except those acquired by escheat or foreclosure

Source: Alaska Statutes, Title 38; Alaska Administrative Code, Title II.

Table 8-4
LAND STATUS
BRISTOL BAY — 1973

Status Category	Acres*
Patented Lands	
Private	8,560
State	87,072
State Selections	
Tentatively Approved	1,190,857
Pending	10,588,130
Native Allotment Applications	132,081
Other Applications	8,492
Indian Reserves	1,376
Military Reservations	2,524
National Monument	1,490,712
Power Site or Project and	
Other Withdrawals	54,681
Land Withdrawn by ANCSA	
Classification and D-1 Lands	1,907,385
D-2 Lands	5,103,669
Wildlife Refuge Replacement	587,324
Village Withdrawal	7,487,599
Village Deficiency	188,981
Regional Deficiency	0
Total Land Acres Withdrawn	28,839,443
Total Land Acres in Region	26,021,012

*Land acres only

Source: U.S. Department of the Interior, Bureau of Land Management, Land
Status Information for Bristol Bay Regional Corporation, July 1973.

Katmai National Monument

Approximately 1.5 million acres of Katmai National Monument are in Bristol Bay. Land use in this area is quite restricted, because the area was originally withdrawn to protect unique geologic features and was later expanded for wildlife habitat protection (Table 8-3). The National Monument is withdrawn from appropriation under the public land laws, location and entry under the mining laws and leasing under the Minerals Leasing Act. No hunting is allowed, but subsistence fishing is permitted along with sport fishing, berry picking, and other recreational uses. The state does not have land selection rights in Katmai National Monument.

Outer Continental Shelf Lands

These lands include the seabed and subsoil beyond the 3-mile territorial limits. The federal government has jurisdiction in this zone to the 200-meter isobath and could claim beyond, if it were capable of exploiting the subsoil and seabed resources.[10]

The laws and regulations which pertain to the other public lands of the United States do not apply to the continental shelf lands. The lands cannot be appropriated and are not open to entry under the mining laws. Geological and geophysical explorations can take place, and oil and gas can be extracted through lease. The U.S. reserves the right to the helium from all gas produced in the area and to fissionable materials such as thorium and uranium.[11]

State- and Private-Patented Lands

State-patented lands total approximately 87,000 acres in the Bristol Bay region. These include state selections to which the state

---

[10]David M. Hickok, and Esther C. Wunicke, *Observations on Marine Affairs in Alaska*; paper prepared for Alaska Commission for Ocean Advancement through Science and Technology (Anchorage: University of Alaska, February 1970) p. 29.

[11]United States Code, Title 43, Section 1331.

has received patent, mineral estate patents, airport conveyances, and quitclaim deeds. The acreage figure shown in Table 8-4 does not include tidelands, submerged lands, and shorelands granted to the state in the Statehood Act.[12] State-patented lands now represent a very small portion of the region, but if all the lands which are tentatively approved or are pending approval are eventually patented, the state would have title to 11.9 million acres, nearly half of the entire region, exclusive of tidal or submerged lands or lands under nontidal, navigable water.

State-patented lands, as well as those tentatively approved by the U.S. government for patent under the Statehood Act, are under the management of the state. These lands first fall into an unclassified status and are subject to eventual classification. The various classfications determine the use permitted. The land-use constraints governing each classification are summarized in Table 8-3. All of the various land categories can be used for purposes "other than for which classified, provided such use is consistent with the public interest."[13]

There are 8,560 acres of private-patented lands in the Bristol Bay region. The owner of the lands determines the use which is to be made of the surface resources of the land and of its subsurface resources if he has subsurface rights. If the subsurface rights are reserved for the government, the owner or someone other than the owner can prospect or explore for oil and gas on the land if he obtains a permit from the government. Because of their small size and scattered nature, private lands are not shown on the maps.

---

[12]Title 11 of the Alaska Administrative Code defines these lands as follows:
Submerged Lands: ". . . . covered by tidal waters between the line of mean low water and seaward to a distance of three geographical miles or further as may hereafter be properly claimed by the state."
Tidelands: " . . . periodically covered by tidal waters between elevation of mean high tide and mean low tide."
Shorelands: " . . . covered by non-tidal waters that are navigable under the laws of the United States up to ordinary highwater mark as modified by accretion, erosion, or reliction."

[13]Alaska Administrative Code, Title 11.

Lands of Indefinite Status

Military reservations and power site withdrawals have an indefinite status. There are approximately 2,500 acres of military reservations in the region. Most of this acreage is contained within the King Salmon Air Force Base. Under provisions of Public Land Order 5187, all military reservations are closed to appropriation, mining, and mineral leasing in order to protect the public interest in the lands for use when the lands are no longer needed for military or defense purposes. Some uses are permitted at the discretion of the agency administering the lands. While any of the area remains a military reservation, the state has no selection rights.

About 55 thousand acres are withdrawn for power sites or projects and other miscellaneous withdrawals. Power sites or power project areas are closed to appropriation under the public land laws, but other uses may be permitted.

Lands with a Temporary Status Classification

State Selected Lands

The state has selected and not yet received patent for a total of 11.8 million acres under provision of the Alaska Statehood Act (Table 8-4). Of this total, 1.2 million acres have been tentatively approved for patent and about 10.6 million acres are pending approval. The location of the tentatively approved and pending acreage are shown on Map 8-1. Under the provisions of ANCSA, each Native village corporation can select up to 69,120 acres or three townships from that state selected or tentatively approved land which was selected before January 17, 1969.[14] There is no upper limit on the acreage that the Native village corporations can select from state selections made after this date. There are approximately twenty-four villages which could select lands from state selections, and the amount each village corporation will select will not be known until after December 18, 1974, the deadline for village selections. State

---

[14]Federal Register Section 2651-4.

lands selected by village corporations will be made up from other land areas, but not necessarily from within Bristol Bay.

Tentatively approved lands are under the management of the state. The lands are also subject to classification and the same land-use constraints as patented state lands. State selected lands which are pending approval are administered by the Secretary of the Interior, who has the authority to make contracts, and issue leases, permits, rights-of-way or easements. Prior to doing any of the above, the Secretary of the Interior would obtain the views of the state. The land uses permitted on these lands can be seen in Table 8-4.

Native Allotment Applications

Native allotment applications do not constitute a land withdrawal in themselves. Under Section 14(h) of ANCSA, a portion of 2 million acres will be conveyed to Alaska Natives throughout the state to cover applications that were applied for under the Native Allotment Acts of 1887, 1906, and 1910 which were repealed by ANCSA. This acreage will also cover additional applications authorized by Section 12(b) of ANCSA which conveys to a Native up to 160 acres of land applied for within two years after the enactment of ANCSA, if this land was a primary place of residence on August 31, 1971. There are 132 thousand acres of allotment applications made prior to and after ANCSA in the Bristol Bay area. The major portion of these are located along the river systems which drain into the northern portion of Bristol Bay (see Map 8-2).

Lands Withdrawn Under Section D-2 of ANCSA

Under Section D-2 of ANCSA, lands were withdrawn for study and for possible recommendations to Congress as additions to or creation as units of one of the "four systems": National Park, National Forest, Wildlife Refuge, or Wild and Scenic River Systems. This withdrawal expires on December 18, 1978. The D-2 lands withdrawn in the region total 5.1 million acres. The land-use constraints for these lands are indicated in Table 8-3.

These lands are currently being reviewed by the Secretary of the

Interior who before December 18, 1973, must submit to Congress legislative proposals for their inclusion in one of the four systems. Lands originally withdrawn under the D-2 classification not recommended for the four systems will be available for selection by the state, regional corporations, and for appropriation under the public land laws. Congress has until December 18, 1978, to act upon the Secretary's recommendations. After this date, lands not so acted upon will be open to state selections and appropriation under the public land laws. Prior to December 18, 1978, ANCSA permits the state and the Native regional corporations to identify D-2 lands desired for selection, but these can only be conveyed if they are not incorporated into the four systems.

The Secretary of the Interior can make contracts and grant leases, permits, rights-of-way or easements. Mineral lease applications will be rejected until the public land order classifying D-2 lands is modified, or the lands are reclassified to permit mineral leasing.

Native Selections Under ANCSA

Lands withdrawn under ANCSA for Native selections also have a temporary status. The following statement from a book of guidelines for land selection under ANCSA explains the Native land selection process for the state as a whole and the role and time limits attached to each withdrawal category:

> The village land selection of 17,000,000 acres for the whole state must be selected from lands designated as: a) village withdrawal area or b) village deficiency land if the regular withdrawal is insufficient. This land is selected by the village corporation. First to be selected are all available lands in the townships in which the village is located. Then additional land is selected based on village enrollment. The minimum entitlement for an incorporated village with an enrollment of at least 25 is three townships. This selection must be completed by December 18, 1974 and will result in surface lands going to residents, businesses, subsistence sites, non-profit organizations, municipal corporations or other selected users. The subsurface rights go to the regional corporation.

> Additional village lands of 5,000,000 acres for the whole state must be selected from lands designated as: a) village with-

drawal area or b) village deficiency land if the regular withdrawal is insufficient. This land is selected by the village corporation following the division of the land among the regional villages based upon subsistence need, historic use and population. The amount of land awarded the region initially is determined by the regional enrollment. This results in the village receiving title to additional surface lands while the region receives title to their subsurface resources.

The regional land selection of 16,000,000 acres for the whole state must be selected from lands designated as: a) village withdrawal lands remaining or b) regional deficiency land if insufficient village withdrawal remains. This land is selected by the regional corporation. Each region's entitlement is based on the size of the region's area with deductions for previous village selection. Land is selected on the basis of the regional corporation's management decisions for the future of the region. This selection must be completed by December 18, 1975 and will result in the land being used according to the regional corporation's plan for the future of the region. Selection from unreserved and unappropriated public lands outside the withdrawal areas of 1,500,000 acres for the whole state must be selected for the preservation of historical places and cemetery sites and residence land for small non-village groups and individuals. Selection of the place of residence for non-village individuals must be completed by December 18, 1973. This will result in the preservation of sites of importance to the region as well as residence land outside the established villages.

Selection of any remaining lands to fulfill the 40 million acre entitlement of the Act must be selected from remaining withdrawal or deficiency lands. The regional corporation selects these lands based on regional enrollment. Through this section the entire 40 million acre entitlement is insured in accordance with the Act.[15]

The land from which Native village corporations and regional corporations can select their entitlement totals approximately 7.8 million acres. Of this, 7.5 million acres are classified as village withdrawals and 0.3 million acres are classified as village deficiency with-

---

[15] University of Alaska, *Village and Regional Land Selection.*

drawals. Under Section 12(a) of ANCSA the following villages are eligible to select land:[16]

	Estimated Land Entitlement
Aleknagik	115,200
Clark Point	92,160
Dillingham	161,280
Egegik	92,160
Ekuk	69,120
Ekwok	92,160
Igiugig	69,120
Iliamna	69,120
Kakhonak	69,120
Koliganek	92,160
Levelock	92,160
Manokotak	115,200
Naknek	115,200
Newhalen	69,120
New Stuyahok	115,200
Nondalton	115,200
Pedro Bay	92,160
Pilot Point	92,160
Portage Creek	69,120
Port Heiden	69,120
South Naknek	92,160
Togiak	115,200
Twin Hills	69,120
Ugashik	69,120

Land-use constraints on land withdrawn for Native selections are given in Table 8-1. After December 18, 1975, most lands not selected by the Native corporations will be classified by the Secretary of the Interior to protect the public interest. The state will have selection rights on most of these lands.

---

[16]The Alaska Native Foundation, *The Alaska Native Management Report* (Anchorage: January 15, 1974) p. 7.

Miscellaneous Land Withdrawals

Lands designated under Section 17(d) (1) of ANCSA and Public Land Orders 5180 and 5186 were withdrawn to determine their proper classification in order to protect the public interest. There are 1.9 million acres of these public interest areas. The land-use constraints imposed on these so-called D-1 lands are similar to those for D-2 lands except that location and entry for metaliferous minerals is permitted on D-1 lands (see Table 8-1). Wildlife refuge replacement lands were withdrawn to serve as possible replacements for existing refuge lands that are selected by the Native village corporations. There are 0.6 million acres in this classification and they are under the same land-use constraints as D-2 lands (see Table 8-1). The Secretary of the Interior is under no time constraints to rescind or reclassify either Section 17(d) (1) or wildlife replacement lands.